Sex and the Supreme Court

Obscenity and Indecency Law in Canada

Richard Jochelson & Kirsten Kramar

Fernwood Publishing • Halifax & Winnipeg

Editing and design:Brenda Conroy
Cover design: John van der Woude
Printed and bound in Canada by Hignell Book Printing

Published in Canada by Fernwood Publishing
32 Oceanvista Lane
Black Point, Nova Scotia, B0J 1B0
and 748 Broadway Avenue, Winnipeg, Manitoba, R3G 0X3
www.fernwoodpublishing.ca

Fernwood Publishing Company Limited gratefully acknowledges the financial support of the
Government of Canada through the Canada Book Fund, the Canada Council for the Arts, the
Nova Scotia Department of Tourism and Culture and the Province of Manitoba, through the
Book Publishing Tax Credit, for our publishing program.

Library and Archives Canada Cataloguing in Publication

Jochelson, Richard, 1974-
Sex and the Supreme Court : obscenity and indecency law
in Canada / Richard Jochelson, Kirsten Kramar,.

(Basics)
Includes bibliographical references.
ISBN 978-1-55266-415-5

1. Obscenity (Law)--Canada. 2. Pornography--Law and
legislation--Canada. 3. Sex and law--Canada. I. Kramar,
Kirsten Johnson, 1965- II. Title. III. Series: Fernwood basics

KE9070.J63 2011   345.71'0274   C2010-908060-2
KF9444.J63 2011

Contents

Acknowledgements

Straddling the fields of both law and social theory is fraught with challenges for those of us who seek to examine the law using the theoretical tools learned outside of a law and society program or law school. Similarly, examining the social effects of law for those with the tools learned inside a law and society program and law school often presents a significant challenge. In our experience, and despite those who worship at the altar of inter-disciplinarity, it has been largely impossible to bridge the gap between social theory and legal activism with respect to obscenity and indecency scholarship. As a consequence of the activist debates of the 1990s, it has proven especially challenging to move beyond advocacy towards theorizing the rationalities that underpin the justifications for power. We believe this is because the activist debates that preceded our research tended to concentrate on redistributing that coercive power in the name of feminism. Whether power is excercised from a conservative, liberal or feminist perspective is not what animates this research. We are interested in examining how power is deployed in the context of human sexuality and in how arguments from different political perspectives have been operationalized historically at the Supreme Court level. Because our project is analytical rather than foundational, we find ourselves at odds with many of our contemporaries — not because we disagree with their political objectives, but because we fundamentally disagree with those academic approaches that seek to promote particular activist political programs. We are, however, committed to the analytical project undertaken by scholars such as Andrew Koppelmen who argue that dangerous ideas are best aired with maximum public debate, rather than left to fester in the closet. Discussing difficult ideas is distinct from promoting those same ideas. We find ourselves without many supporters when we seek to promote *scholarship* in which difficult ideas about sexual freedom are debated and defended. These include the observation that power is sometimes deployed tyrannically in liberal democracies to promote freedom *and* equality for women and other historically marginalized groups. This is not a popular academic idea when victims' rights discourses drive academic scholarship — which has sometimes become indecipherable from activist causes.

We both want to thank our colleagues in the law and society community for their helpful comments and questions during conferences presentations, in particular, Brenda Cossman, Karen Crawley and William Watson. We also want to thank Anna Jochelson and Robert Kramar, who supported our many hours away from home on the weekends, and our respective children, Leah Jochelson, Emily Jochelson, Mieka Kramar and Evie Kramar, who endured late dinners and lost playtime. Thank you also to Melanie Murchison and Tess Klachefsky for logistical support.

Thank you also to Fernwood Publishing, in particular our friends Jessica Antony and Wayne Antony, for their support of our work. We have been given the freedom to think through some very difficult and unpopular ideas with the support of a publishing team committed to Canadian academic scholarship rather than the commercialization of academic scholarship. Thanks also to the other Fernwood people involved in the production of this book: Brenda Conroy, Debbie Mathers and Beverley Rach.

Preface

Five years after the Supreme Court restated the test for obscenity and indecency under the *Criminal Code* of Canada and almost twenty years since it considered whether sexually explicit materials could be obscene in Canada, questions about the use of censorship to limit freedom of expression has now extended to Zombieland. Rémy Couture, who is a "Montreal-based special-effects artist, photographer and maker of short horror films" has been charged under section 163 of Canada's *Criminal Code*, which deals with child pornography. These charges were laid after Interpol was alerted by someone in Germany who viewed the images of zombie-sex online. The horror films in question showed zombies engaged in sexual contexts, some of whom appeared to be under the age of eighteen, thereby triggering the police to lay a charge under the child pornography provision. In this regard, those obscenity legal scholars who argue that academic or political interest in obscenity and indecency is no longer necessary because the police have moved on to child pornography enforcement, may be indeed correct. But, these commentators are correct only insofar as they limit their interests to the prosecutorial effects of law. Of course, laws that empower the state to censor and punish its citizens have much wider reaching effects because they communicate ideas to the wider society in which they operate about the limits of acceptable conduct and the justifications for state intervention. They may also cause us to modify our sexual expression and conduct in particular ways to as to conform to a particular legal conception of right and wrong, or good and bad. In other words, unexamined law that creates fixed norms to which we unknowingly or unwittingly conform means we may be silently governed without examining the roots of that governance structure. This book is about examining that governance structure.

Academics have debated justifications for censorship and the limits of free expression when it comes to pornography and other forms of sexually explicit materials and practices for centuries. The pairing of sex and violence has always been maligned. Sex and violence is the principal target of the obscenity provision's ire (sex coupled with violence is one of the enumerated examples of the "undue" exploitation of sex under the *Criminal Code*). The lack of critical attention to the ongoing issues raised by the obscenity debate, particularly in the context of sexually explicit adult speech and conduct, may largely stem from the fact that feminist and queer[1] activists successfully challenged the law and its discriminatory application through the major constitutional cases dealing with obscenity in the twentieth century. By the end of the twentieth century in Canada, obscenity laws were less rooted in conservative moral values and less discriminatory towards queer pornography.

As such, there has been virtually no critical analysis of the Supreme Court decision in *R. v. Labaye* [2005], in which the Court essentially legalized private swingers clubs and their alternative sexual practices, thus beginning an era of the liberalization of laws that have historically limited sexual expression and conduct when they fail to conform to monogamous heterosexual norms. Yet, despite the purported liberalization of Canadian sex laws, zombie horror film producers such Rémy Couture continue to attract state sanction. Distaste for artistic zombie-porn involving teenaged victims (or put in other terms, morality) may continue to underpin the sensibilities of those who enforce the Canadian obscenity laws.[2] The example of the Couture prosecution is interesting because it is the first time the Canadian courts will consider whether "horror" in a sexual context can be obscene. What is different about this case is that the dominant depictions involved "horror" rather than "sex" along with the red herring of so-called "children."[3]

One can certainly empathize with *Globe and Mail* journalist Russell Smith, who notes: "Remy Couture's violent videos are dumb, but that's not illegal" (Smith 2010). What remains in the wake of prosecutions of these sorts, as well as the laws used to punish people, have broader effects on the Canadian population. For this reason, and regardless of the outcome of the case, we believe that it is an example of why, more than ever, we need to understand how Canadian law governs indecency and obscenity law and why the discussion and a review of the recent legal history has ramifications and relevance as we move forward. As you navigate the often dense, rhetorical, historical, legal and philosophical material covered in this book, remember that the abstractions with which we engage may be given life by actual cases. The Couture prosecution for making "zombie porn" is one such example.

Notes

1. We use the term queer to refer to people who identify themselves as gay, lesbian, bisexual, questioning, transgendered, transsexual, two spirited and/or intersexed.

2. Indeed an analysis of lower court cases that cite *Labaye* in their reasoning over the last five years demonstrates that the issue of indecency and obscenity remains very much alive for Canadian courts. A search into cases that have considered *Labaye* since the beginning of 2010 reveals over twenty reported cases, not including unpublished decisions or other occasions where law enforcement has levelled obscenity or indecency charges.

3. The issue of child pornography is beyond the scope of this book because it engages a host of discussions that are particular to the legislative framework and academic research and debates about the regulation of sexually explicit images involving children. This includes the very meaning of what it is to be a "child," issues pertaining to the trafficking of children and artistic representations of children in sexual contexts including works of fiction that do not actually involve children and the "harms" inherent in possessing these works of fiction. This merits a book length analysis. For a recent example, see Ost (2009).

Chapter One

Theoretical Debates

Harm in the Context of Obscenity and Indecency Law in Canada

This book traces the socio-legal history of the criminalization of both pornography[1] and "bawdy houses"[2] in Canada. Our aim is to provide an historical awareness of our present circumstance with respect to the Canadian law of obscenity and indecency and to show that contemporary norms produced in law around obscene and indecent sexual practices and commodities are very much shaped by the past. Despite the implementation of the *Charter of Rights and Freedoms* in 1982, the rationality underpinning obscenity (criminalized sexually explicit expression) and indecency (criminalized sexually explicit conduct) laws has shifted only marginally since Confederation in 1867. Indeed, it may be argued that the "calculus," or process, for determining whether something is obscene or indecent, has not changed at all. Instead, what has changed is what is perceived to cause harm. Harm is liberalism's justification for using the power of the state to criminalize.

Our empirical focus is on how the state works out the tension between liberty (as self-government) and coercion (as non-liberal exercise of power) in, and through, the courts' justifications for interfering in the sexual lives of its citizens through censorship and criminal sanction. Contemporary jurisprudence of obscenity and indecency is working out tensions inherent to liberalism; the tensions between sexual freedom as a form of self-government, market freedom, including the freedom to manufacture, distribute and profit from the consumption of commoditized sexually explicit materials and services, and state sanction. These tensions also sometimes support justifications for censorship and criminal sanction when sexual self-government is presumed to have a negative impact on women in a society characterized by the constitutional commitment to equality as guaranteed by section 15 of the *Charter*. We trace the legal authorities, techniques and lines of state force that are deployed where competing discourses of liberty and coercion both contest and defend governmental strategies (Rose and Valverde

1998: 541). We locate our analysis in other criticisms of liberalism, or what has come to be known as "neoliberalism," with the goal of understanding how obscenity and indecency jurisprudence creates sexual subjects through relations of power and subjugation. Keep in mind from the outset that criminal obscenity/indecency law is only one source of subjugation that influences sexual subjectivity and that the state also implements other techniques of constraint (Foucault 1997: 266).

Beginning roughly in late 1980s, the pornography industry has flourished under the so-called "free market" conditions of neoliberalism, which characterizes Western liberal democracies. Angela Harris summarizes neoliberalism as follows:

> Neoliberalism entails a commitment to the dismantling of the economic arrangements sometimes called "Fordism," and their replacement with an economy driven by substantially deregulated markets (themselves driven by the interests of corporate and finance capital), an economy in which capital's upper hand over labour has led to dramatically increasing inequalities of income and wealth. Neoliberalism also entails the dismantling of state institutions meant to cushion citizens against economic risk, and an approach to governance that favors "privatization," "deregulation," and other policies that transfer political power from governments to markets. Finally, neoliberalism entails a series of social projects (often described as "culture wars") that address the anxieties of the increasingly economically precarious and politically disempowered middle and working classes by constructing a sentimentalized vision of the innocent yet victimized, taxpaying, suburban good citizen and then attacking that citizen's purported enemies — reliably, queers, liberals, feminists, and blacks; episodically, Asians and immigrants; and most recently people (in the United States and abroad) who "hate America." Neoliberalism, then, is a complex set of projects that operate simultaneously on economic, political and cultural fronts. Not surprisingly, neoliberalism has also entailed significant changes in legal thought and practice. (Harris 2006: 1541–42).

Part of our aim in this book is also to understand obscenity and indecency law as a important feature of sexual citizenship and a reflection of sexual values inherent to North American liberalism.

Liberalism has created the fiction of "free" markets by choosing when and where to focus government intervention. Neoliberalism is said to be much more "laissez-faire" than early to mid-twentieth-century forms of liberalism, which focused on social welfare spending. When this form of spending declined, a concomitant increase in economic inequalities (particularly for non-whites and women in the former Soviet Union and Eastern bloc states, particularly the Balkans) fuelled the rapid expansion of the sex trade industry (Malarek 2003). This time period witnessed the dismantling of the welfare state in Canada, the U.S. and Britain, along with the upward distribution of social and economic resources to the wealthy. The widespread use of computers in the home and the implementation of infrastructure to provide each and every household with cheap and easy access to the Internet further expanded what is now largely a cyber-porn market and sex trade industry. According to *Macleans* (Polak 2008: 37), "the North American cyber-porn industry brings in about 2 billion dollars per year." Online pornography is easily accessible and virtually unregulated. In Canada, no corporation has ever been convicted (or perhaps even charged) with possessing or distributing "obscenity." Successive Canadian governments have viewed this pornography market as something that should not be subject to state intervention, well in keeping with neoliberalism's transfer of power from governments to markets. Thus, the state constitutes the commodified sex trade as outside of politics and therefore operating within that "private" space that does not belong to government. Only when private individuals complain to the authorities are prosecutions likely to be launched, as we saw in the case of Montreal "zombie-porn" maker, Rémy Couture. As a result, these prosecutions are *ad hoc* and highly individualized.

Liberalism has developed its legal technologies for intervening into the terrain of "the social," defined as the "public" sphere, when unruly subjects fail to self-govern in a manner consistent with its vision of a well ordered, properly functioning society (what we term a functionalist account). But this intervention is mainly, if not entirely, directed at the sexual conduct of *individuals*. To the extent that governments have adopted a largely laissez-faire approach to the regulation of the porn industry (and we are not arguing that they should or should not), the notion of "the social" with respect to the sex trade has largely disappeared (Rose 1999).

As part of an overall political project, our aim is to take up Harris's (2006: 1581) challenge to "'politicize' (that is, make visible the politics already hidden but already within) the 'private' sphere." In order to achieve this politicization, we provide a description of the governmental rationales and techniques following the Supreme Court decision in *R. v. Labaye* — the largely ignored Canadian case which ruled that a popular swingers club in Montreal was not an indecent bawdy house under the *Criminal Code*. The *Labaye* case is particularly interesting because it re-defined the judicial test for establishing indecency and obscenity in Canada. In the process it revealed the longstanding rationale for criminal intervention in the context of the laws of sexual expression and conduct.

We show how early obscenity cases enforced religious and class-based morality, while later cases focused on community standards of tolerance and the furtherance of normative political objectives. These earlier cases were in response to the state's attempts at repressing sexually explicit materials that satirized and sexualized religious figures or made any references to homosexuality, as well as materials that provided education about reproduction and birth control.

Later, in the twentieth century and throughout the post-*Charter* era, liberals and feminists were critical of the justifications for censorship adopted by judges, seeing them as forms of *moral* regulation. Their criticisms were levelled mainly on liberal and various feminist grounds in reaction to the conservative religious- and class-based justifications for censorship. In response, conservatives reacted negatively to the liberal and feminist criticisms on the grounds that theirs was too liberal (or too feminist) an approach for dealing with sexually explicit materials, largely because such materials could corrupt the morals of the unruly consumer (Johnson 1995). Now with the apparently neutral language of "harm" and "risk of harm," the Court continues to use political values to justify censorship of obscenity and the criminalization of indecency in a manner that may satisfy all its critics across the political spectrum. The Supreme Court decision in *R. v. Labaye* created a seemingly "objective" test for criminalizing obscenity and indecency by reconfiguring the harms-based obscenity test established in *R. v. Butler* [1992].[3] The decision has been positively received and seen by some commentators as a victory for liberalism and feminism in both Canada and the United States (Boyce 2008; Craig 2008, 2009).

Law and the Censorship of Obscenity
In the nineteenth century, the Victorians associated non-monogamous and non-heterosexual sexuality with "vice" leading to the corruption of morals. The Victorians regulated these non-normative sexualities through a religious- and class-focused application of criminal law on the grounds that unconventional sexuality caused moral harm to those susceptible to depravity and corruption, which meant especially those at the "bottom" of the social hierarchy. These "depraved and corrupted" groups were in turn understood to harm society as a whole. This perceived corruption of morals undermined the proper functioning of society during the Victorian era, and courts sought to steer society in the direction of achieving moral equilibrium or homeostatic perfection. This functionalist project has remained to the present day (Johnson 1995).[4]

Courts continue to presume that sexually explicit imagery and unconventional and commercial sex practices cause harm to the fabric of society. State intervention through criminalization which places limitations on freedom of expression, in the classic justification for obscenity and indecency laws, is for the purpose of preventing this general moral harm. This is equally a strategy for normalizing sexual practices and attitudes. Protecting the moral fabric of society is the principal justification for both obscenity and indecency laws, one that can be traced back to early obscenity cases. The purported aim of obscenity and indecency law is to protect us from the negative attitudes created by sexually explicit publications and unconventional and commercial sex practices as well from as the affront to certain kinds of constitutionally enshrined political values such as liberty and equality. The regulation of the sex trade through indecency law is largely based on the notion that public sex is a public nuisance because it exposes non-consenting populations to sexually explicit activities — that it disrupts the prevailing social order (Jochelson 2009a, 2009b).

Our analysis demonstrates that the social demands for equality and civil rights with respect to sexual expression of the 1980s and 1990s of the various feminists and gay, lesbian, bi-sexual and trans-gendered (GLBT) movements have been translated into obscenity and indecency jurisprudence by the Supreme Court decision in *R. v. Labaye* in a manner that re-brands liberalism to make it both feminist and queer friendly.[5] This façade of friendliness masks an insipid variant of freedom because it empowers the new "risk of harm" test for obscenity and indecency. As Valverde argues in relation to earlier indecency cases, the legal categories of "harm" and "risk of harm" "[act] as veritable joker cards that can serve completely different purposes depending on the context" (1999: 184). The harm test articulated in *Labaye* is presented *by the Court* as a more sophisticated test for harm, rooted in objectivity and empiricism. However, we show, through an examination of indecency cases following the *Labaye* decision, that harm and risk of harm are fluid categories that carry with them no consistent or pragmatic meaning. These categories are empty containers ready to be filled. According to Valverde (1999: 184):

> The religious right can read their moral concerns onto "risk of harm," since they believe pornography is harmful to the soul; modernizing actuarial types can breathe a sigh of relief upon hearing that risk is being acknowledged; and feminists can also, on their part, feel pleased that what they think of as the harms of pornography are finally recognized.

These categories are represented as objective but allow for the deployment of political moral value judgments, which in turn create categories of sexual danger and sexual health. Our analysis of *Labaye* also demonstrates that the Court's imposition of particular value judgments about dangerous sexuality using harm and risk of harm inscribe a vision of a consensual moral order to be protected by the work of courts. This vision is always being "protected" in variable ways. The categories of sexual danger are always in a process of (re)construction and often communicate normative ideas about sexual self-regulation. They also can carve out that space deemed private (private property, the market, etc.) into which the state cannot venture when courts decide jurisdictional issues. Thus, determinations of what is sexually dangerous versus sexually healthy (which *are* political) have become dependent upon the predilections of a particular judge, in a particular court, in a particular context, and function like "veritable joker cards" just as Valverde predicted. That these judgments are represented as "objective" simply reveals the Court's faux empiricism — the harm test still depends on the judge's views, regardless of its roots in constitutional values like liberty or equality.

Any deviation from the norm imposed by the Court requires penal intervention as a mode of correction to preserve its own vision of a properly functioning society. This deviation is delineated by the *Labaye* Court as a type of "harm" to be avoided. In the context of the indecency and obscenity debate, the concept of "harm" has been central to the criminalization of acts or speech of a sexual nature.

Liberalism and Harm

The starting point for understanding how harm is understood by the courts in the context of obscenity and indecency rests on the liberal principle that a government ought not intrude in the lives of the citizen, unless it acts to prevent harm to an individual or society. While a seemingly simple creation, defining what is, and is not, harmful is highly contingent upon the context and other variables. It is an established liberal philosophical principle that materials that cause *offence* and even extreme *offence* to one's moral or political values ought not be censored by the state (Feinberg 1985). In other words, being offended by a mere idea or practice engaged in by others in a liberal democratic society is, on this philosophical reading of harm, no justification for state coercion into the lives of its citizens. Therefore, for some liberals, being offended, or having one's morals challenged, is not a justification for censorship because offence falls short of a threshold of harm required to trigger the coercive power of the state. Those who argue for this threshold often point to tangible harms (such as physical harms to participants) as the litmus test for state intervention. Of course this is not a fixed understanding of harm, but it is nonetheless used regularly to justify state intervention. Those who argue that evil ideas (which may or may not lead to evil deeds) ought to be justification for criminal sanction are firmly in the *offence* category of harm. In both Canadian and U.S. law, the criminalization of obscenity is anomalous because constitutional protection extends to all sorts of speech that is unpopular, offensive and even harmful. For example, Hitler's *Mein Kampf* (1925/1926) and Karl Marx's *Das Kapital* (1867, Eng. trans. 1887) contained ideas that, through the incitement of action, caused considerable harm to millions of people.

According to Koppelman (2005, 2008), the idea that morally repugnant literature results in morally repugnant fixed norms is not a matter that obscenity law can fix. Koppelman argues that even if obscene materials promote bad fixed norms, "nothing about its effects on its readers necessarily follows from this fact" (2008: 122). In other words, for Koppelman, the focus on sexual objectification and the eroticization of cruelty as the moral harm of pornography cannot ground the arguments for censorship firmly in a liberal harm principle, because these claims about pornography tell us nothing about its actual effects on readers. Advocates of this position point out that social scientific research on the connection between pornography and violence against women is weak and inconclusive, sometimes showing limited long-term effects, if any (for other examples, see Cossman 2003; Sumner 2004).[6] This sort of research has never been able to sort out the interactive effects of broader already existing societal norms concerning women's sexuality. Put succinctly, study of the causal effect of exposure to obscene materials has yielded results that are equivocal, and liberal philosophers generally believe that the causal case for harm has not been made. Rather than viewing the effects as harmful, certain liberal scholars contend at most that the effect of our exposure to obscene material is some kind of damage to our conception of how a society ought to function. In this regard, liberals generally are unsupportive of the legal idea that exposure to sexually explicit materials results in verifiable harm to our attitudes about women and thus undermine societal values. From this perspective, to suggest that the state *must* intervene to criminalize obscenity that is harmful to attitudes is to assume that obscenity short-circuits our ability to conduct a rational assessment of sexually explicit and other morally offensive materials.

This resistance to paternalism is evident in the early works of classical liberalism. According to liberal doctrine, since at least the writings of Mill (1869), the state has been justified in curtailing its citizens' liberty *only* to protect others from harm. In *On Liberty*, John Stuart Mill explored the legitimate exercise of societal power on the individual (Mill 1869: para. 9). His argument was that "the only purpose for which power can be rightfully exercised over any member of a civilized community, against his will, is to prevent harm to others; his own good, either physical or moral, is not a sufficient warrant" (1869: para. 9). From this perspective, citizens in a liberal democratic society have the intrinsic freedom to express hateful or obscene (morally evil) ideas mainly because free speech plays an important role in democratic societies. This "democratic" argument against coercion of unpopular, offensive or harmful expression holds that within the realm of public speech, freedom is absolute; for liberals democratic governance requires free and open speech as a matter of self governance. People need free speech "because they have decided, in adopting, maintaining, and interpreting their Constitution, to govern themselves rather than to be governed by others" (Meiklejohn 1961: XX). This aligns with the liberal contention that more speech rather than less speech is the prescription to solving the problems inherent in controversial expression. For instance, Strossen writes that "a central tenet of... free speech jurisprudence: [is] that the appropriate antidote to speech with which we disagree, or offends us, is more speech" (Strossen 1995: 1168).

A further liberal rationale against censorship and in defence of freedom of speech is connected to the right of citizens to autonomy. From this perspective, autonomy requires personal sovereignty in determining what to believe and in weighing competing reasons for action; when the state intervenes to make those choices it behaves in an illiberal manner. The autonomy-based account of free speech focuses on the individual involved in a speech event, whether it be the speaker or the listener. Any argument in favour of censorship that is based on the idea that morally repugnant ideas cause harm, including the formation of false beliefs about women and harmful acts as a result of those beliefs, is a form of tyranny. Even where a causal link may be established between the promotion of false beliefs and morally repugnant ideas, liberals argue that the state interferes with our autonomy when it intervenes to criminalize morally undesirable ideas (Scanlon 1972: 758–59). Therefore, if the government interferes with our freedom to consume sexually explicit materials that present humans in degrading or violent sexual activities, they violate our freedom to determine *for ourselves* whether or not the materials are morally repugnant. In any free society, individuals must be treated sufficiently so as to be capable of forming and acting "upon intelligent conceptions of how their lives should be lived" (Dworkin 1978: 272). This aligns with Mill's (1869) concerns that the pursuit of truth, while important as a justification for free expression, is but one fundamental political concern. Mill (1869) also argued that multiple viewpoints enhance judgment and intellect. For Mill (1869), the pacification of the mind is one consequence of censorship. Free speech, even if it conveys "evil" ideas, are important acts of communication because the public debate that often results from morally evil ideas nevertheless enhances "knowledge, friendship, and self-government" and other socially and politically valuable activities (Mill 1869: 19; Moon 2000).

Koppleman articulates these traditional liberal ideas in a modern context, pointing out that that censorship of "evil" ideas (i.e., through suppressing "objectionable" materials such as hardcore pornography) "dulls" societies *towards* evil because "evil is rarely committed by mustache-twirling villains. More often it is done by people who have succeeded in weaving an elaborate tissue of self-justification, so well-crafted that it completely masks the reality of what they are doing to other people" (2006: 70). In other words, in order to learn about evil we cannot permit our governments to censor it. Koppelman cites Azar Nafisi's *Reading Lolita in Tehran* to buttress his argument. In discussing the dictatorship of Ayatollah Ruhollah Khomeini, Nafisi writes that "Islamic fundamentalism called for micromanaging the lives of everyone and of women in particular" which included banning Western texts like *Lolita* (Koppelman 2006: 68).[7] For Nafisi, the value in reading such texts lies in "a parallel between what Humbert tried to do to Lolita and what Kohmeini tried to do to his subjects: both involve 'the confiscation of one individual's life by another'" (Koppelman 2006: 68). Because the text teaches us about the parallels between Islamic dictators and sexual dictators, "the portrayals of evil such as occur in *Lolita* are risky, but morally valuable, precisely because they help to dispel the comfortable notion that evil is wholly other. That notion tends to beget the thought that what we are doing cannot possibly be evil, since we are the ones who are doing it" (Koppelman 2006: 68). In other words, there is profound educational value to be had in the wide dissemination of morally evil ideas.[8]

These liberal accounts of free expression have provided ammunition for the rejection of the feminist governmental rationalities that animate the argument in favour of censorship in order to foster women's equality. Other liberals moderate their positions regarding censorship, viewing sexual speech and activities not as absolute but rather as actionable when a certain threshold of "harm" is met, that is, some activities or expression could be limited in the service of avoiding harm. These moderated liberal viewpoints require more than the mere assertion of harm or risk of harm and look for something more tangible upon which to justify state intervention. For instance, some would argue that sexual expression should only be limitable when its effects amount to the willful promotion of hatred against women (Jochelson 2009a; Sumner 2004; Ryder 2001). Anti-pornography feminists tend to equate harms to women's equality as ammunition for suppressing sexual activity and expression. These claims fall short of the harmful links sought by moderated liberals, but nonetheless, the analytics of harm as a justification for state suppression has provided powerful fuel for many anti-pornography activists (Jochelson 2009a, 2009b).

The Mutant Harm Principle

The following chapters show that the *Labaye* Court has articulated a justification for censorship of obscenity and criminalization of indecency that is not confined to a single logic. By shifting the test away from the values and opinions of the "community" to the abstract values of liberalism, the new test can easily be read in multiple directions including a feminist one. This approach has been embraced by those who want to use the power of the state to promote women's equality (Craig 2009). In this book, we wrestle with the way in which the harm principle has been used to justify censorship in the context of obscenity and indecency. Liberals have criticized the use of the harm principle by the state and other administrative bodies to justify censorship on the basis of *"feeling* subordinated or *feeling* silenced [by obscenity and/or indecency] which in turn [is] inextricably bound up with feeling put upon, outraged or offended, at which point we may approach moralism of the old sort" (Green 2000: 29, emphasis in original). Criticisms are also levied against the use of the harm principle to justify state sanction when it is used to censor sexually explicit materials which are said to cause harm, whether it be direct or indirect harm. We argue that judges continue to operationalize "moralism of the old sort"; on some occasions they even do so "in the name of feminism," which we find interesting.

Currently, in Canadian law, criminalization is legitimized by the courts in relation to the kinds of harm, or risk of harm, caused by obscenity and indecency. Harm is framed chiefly as "harm to society," a category that includes harm to women and men, affronts to our personal liberties and damage done to other constitutional values such as equality (Jochelson 2009a, 2009b). Valverde (1999) describes such harms as multi-vocal, which illustrates the multiple affected perspectives of the targets and participants of sexual speech and conduct. We argue that in Canada, the test, while wearing a veil of multiplicity of contexts, has actually been cloaked in terms of the "proper functioning of society." The multi-vocality observed by some scholars has been subsumed under a broader category of harm which the courts see themselves as tasked with preventing — a category we call "societal harm." Harm to women, harm to men and harm to political values such as liberty and equality have historically been deployed to constitute a consensual moral order — a uni-vocal goal.

Nevertheless, we agree with Valverde that the characterization of Canadian sex laws as a "relatively smooth progress towards modernization and rationalization" is a narrative "without foundation" (Valverde 1999: 182). Indeed, any attempts to read a new found liberalization and/or feminism into the law of obscenity and indecency are illusory post-*Labaye*. We argue throughout this book that the elimination of the voices of sexual communities from judicial decision-making about what counts as *bad* sex (and by extension what counts as *good* sex) is a development that took place gradually but which reached fruition when the Supreme Court retired its community standards of tolerance test in *Labaye*, replacing it with the harm test as the determining factor in whether obscenity or indecency has occurred.

The use of harm as defined by the *Labaye* Court selects for a universalizing "political morality of harm," which erases the potential for context-based sexual discourses based on diverse experiences. Since at least the passage of the Canadian *Charter of Rights and Freedoms* in 1982, diverse voices were heard as formal legal interveners in Supreme Court cases, offering arguments in the context of constitutional litigation. We explore why those voices have been all but silenced following the decision in *R. v. Labaye*. Before we proceed though, it is vital that we briefly review the most common arguments in the censorship debate in recent Canadian history. This includes, most saliently (often because of their involvement in the litigation), prominent feminist accounts of obscenity in the Canadian context.

The Censorship Debate

One important issue with respect to obscenity has to do with the question of whether pornography is "speech." Both feminist and conservative commentators have argued that pornography is not speech, viewing it instead as something different, which causes direct (participatory) and indirect (equality based, or morally corruptive) harms (MacKinnon 1987). Conservatives have argued that obscene pornography ought to be censored to protect patriarchal values, whereas anti-pornography feminists have argued that obscene pornography ought be censored to protect women and more abstractly women's equality (Jochelson 2009a, 2009b). However, the notion that pornography is not a form of "speech" has been largely discredited (Koppelman 2005, 2006, 2008), a matter that Canadian case law has clearly revealed as well (see for example, *Butler* [1992]).

In the contemporary Canadian constitutional era, this criminalization of both obscenity and indecency is justified to protect a society that claims to be committed to preserving liberty and equality, and it is not unusual for the criminalization of pornography and prostitution to be justified as necessary to protect women's equality. However, where feminists seek to promote women's equality in an inherently unequal society, the courts have taken a much different approach. Courts view society as *threatened* by the existence of obscenity and seek to control it as a way of protecting a "properly functioning society," which is not characterized by social inequality (Johnson 1999). In particular, courts imagine women and men as approaching a properly functioning society as equal subjects, and a society without obscenity and indecency supports this world order. Thus, in deploying the harm test, courts see themselves as moving society away from or inoculating society from the possibility of a "transient pathological state." They see their role as selecting for moral equilibrium or homeostatic perfection. Importantly, this homeostasis assumes a baseline equality of its subjects; the repudiation of obscenity returns the subjects back to the equal baseline. This model of society is quite at odds with the model that underpins most feminist debates in respect of pornography and censorship. A feminist argument would avoid constructions of a "proper society," which are rooted in the idea of an unruly class of morally corruptible innocents — a notion steeped in its own brand of patriarchal hetero-normativity, about which many feminists remain deeply suspicious. In particular, most feminist perspectives would conceive that men and women rarely approach a legal contest as equal subjects (Cossman et al. 1997).

The test for obscene pornography established in *R. v. Butler* by the Supreme Court in 1992 was the first constitutional challenge to the obscenity provisions of the *Criminal Code*. The obscenity provision was upheld by the *Butler* Court on the grounds that "obscene" pornography is harmful to society and therefore its criminalization is justified to protect society. The *Butler* Court continued to rely upon a community standards of tolerance test, in keeping with the case law since the 1950s, when the current obscenity provision was passed. The Court constructed harmful sexual expression as materials which the average Canadian would not or could not imagine other Canadians viewing. The relevant section of the *Criminal Code*, section 163, criminalizes any sexually explicit materials (pornography) as obscene where "a dominant characteristic of the matter or thing is the undue exploitation of sex, violence, crime, horror, cruelty or the undue degradation of the human person." Therefore, the criminal law connects obscenity with the undue exploitation or the undue degradation of the human person and aims to prevent these harms on the grounds that they undermine society's proper functioning. We show that *Labaye* is a continuation, even a strengthening, of this functionalist project.

In practical political and legal terms, lobby groups like the Canadian Civil Liberties Association (CCLA)[9] have sought to protect freedom of expression in cases dealing with sexually explicit materials, while feminist advocacy organizations like the Women's Legal Education and Action Fund (LEAF) have sought to protect equality rights for women.[10] Conservative religious lobbies such as Winnipeg-based, GAP (Group Against Pornography) are opposed to both liberal and certain feminist positions on the state's role in regulating sexually explicit materials seeing a much stronger role for the state.[11] Similarly, Muslim religious groups, such as the Canadian Council of Muslim Women (CCMW), believe that the state ought to criminalize most forms of pornography and other sexually explicit materials.[12] They share a conservative belief that pornography undermines the religious value placed upon heterosexual monogamy and the nuclear family and that pornography promotes the sexual abuse of women and girls.

It is commonly accepted in some feminist circles that anti-pornography feminists have framed their arguments in much of the same language as moral conservatives in respect of pornographic expression (Cossman et al. 1997). According to Gotell (1997: 64):

It is important to recognize that while anti-pornography feminists have condemned the moral-conservative foundations of Canadian obscenity law, they do not reject the notion that law should be used to ensure some form of moral order. The feminist campaign against pornography seeks to reform and recast the moral foundations of law to incorporate a normative concern for sexual harm. In accepting the moral-regulatory function of law, and in other significant respects, anti-pornography feminism thus enters into an uneasy rhetorical and political alliance with the moral right.

Anti-pornography feminists often ground their moral position in harm, by focusing on the deleterious effects of pornography on women in society (for example, see Benedet 2001; Cole 1989; Dworkin 1998; MacKinnon 1987; Mahoney 1991). From this feminist perspective, violent, degrading and dehumanizing sexually explicit materials harm women, as well as the targeted (male) audience, having a negative influence on society at large. This view of sexually explicit expression derives from a basic fear of the current world order as dangerous. In broad terms, these feminists view the world as fraught with the potential to seriously harm women and women's position in society. Thus sexually explicit expression represents several threats. It threatens to undermine gravely the strides that feminists have made towards equality by rehashing misogynistic sexual roles and thereby discrediting certain "radical" feminist work in respect of achieving true equality of the sexes. The threat is also narrow towards those participating in the production of sexually explicit expression. The harms to women include "dehumanization, humiliation, sexual exploitation, forced sex, forced prostitution, physical injury, child sexual abuse and sexual harassment... [the harm] diminishes the reputation of women as a group, deprives women of their credibility and social and self worth, and undermines women's equal access to protected rights." (*R. v. Butler* [1992] 1 S.C.R. 452 at 7.)

For these feminists, sexually explicit expression may not be merely a mirror of the unequal treatment that society fosters between men and women; it may well be one of the root causes of inequality. In this respect, "pornography is a grave social problem, harmful to women and a cause of social decline, and together they pressured political actors for new regulatory responses" (Gotell 1997: 65). Therefore, they seek equality for womankind on the one hand and censoring the threat to that equality on the other hand; in the case of sexually explicit expression, such views may connote complete silencing of pornographic expression rather than dialogue (Dworkin 1998; Mahoney 1991; MacKinnon 1987; Moon 2000).

Anti-pornography activists and scholars, whether conservative (Muslim-conservative or Christian-conservative) or feminist, argue that pornography causes harm to women. Like the Christian and Muslim conservative women's groups, Phyllis Schafley, an American conservative political activist and constitutional law attorney, argues that pornography is a tool for the abuse of women because it causes men to think about women and girls as sexual playthings, which undermines the heterosexual monogamous nuclear family. Schafley and the other conservatives do not think that men would think this way about women and girls if it were not for pornographic imagery circulating freely in society. Schafley and the religious critics also argue that pornography provokes sexual violence and for this reason ought to be strongly policed by the state (Koppelman 2008: 105–106). Although Schafley's position is decidedly anti-feminist, there are strands of agreement about the effects of pornography amongst anti-feminists and anti-pornography feminists. Canadian anti-pornography activists such as Susan Cole (1989), Janine Benedet (2001), and the Canadian women's legal lobby group LEAF argue for strong state policing of pornography because it harms women directly in its production, and harms women indirectly in its free circulation in that it caused men to change their attitudes about women and girls, contributing to their inequality. The anti-pornography feminists disagree with the conservative position that pornography undermines the heterosexual monogamous nuclear family. They also disagree with the liberal position that pornography is a form of expression that ought to be minimally protected under the *Charter of Rights and Freedoms* (Benedet 2001), viewing many forms of pornography as an expression of hatred towards women (MacKinnon 1987). Anti-pornography feminists demand in many cases that the state respond with criminal sanction to the production, distribution and sale of sexually explicit imagery that is violent and/or degrading and dehumanizing to women. Proponents of both the conservative and anti-pornography feminist positions were nominally satisfied by the Court's decision in *R. v. Butler*. As Cossman (1997) and Gotell (1997: 50–51) both argue, this agreement is "rooted in the *Butler* Court's subtle and careful grafting of anti-pornography feminist claims onto more traditional moral-conservative discourses about sexual representation."

American anti-pornography feminists Andrea Dworkin and Catharine MacKinnon also argue that pornography causes sexual harm to women both in its production and because of its circulation in society. However, they view pornography as a violation of American women's civil right to be free from harm and attempted to use civil rights law, rather than appeal to the state through criminal law, to control offensive, harmful sexually explicit materials. Defining pornography as a civil rights violation would allow American women who have been harmed by pornography to sue producers and distributors for civil pecuniary damages, thereby giving women themselves direct redress through punitive damages awards from the courts. In contrast, the Canadian approach would provide a societal remedy through the incarceration of persons charged under the obscenity statute upheld in *R. v. Butler*. Both of these approaches rely on a paradigm that views obscenity as harmful to women and see legal remedies (civil or criminal) as a means of addressing harm (Johnson 1995).

Anti-pornography feminists advocate the use of law to prevent harm to women whilst promoting women's equality (Cole 1989). They view pornography as harmful to women in three distinct ways: it harms actual women in its production; it desensitizes boys and men to sexual violence against women whilst encouraging women to understand themselves as sexual objects; and it contributes to sex discrimination of women amongst broader segments of society by causing negative attitudinal changes in the population at large (Cole 1989; MacKinnon 1987, 2003). It is apparent that, despite differences in the moral imperatives that gave birth to the philosophies, anti-pornography feminist and conservative arguments share many commonalities in terms of their legal approach towards pornography. This position was given legal effect by the Supreme Court of Canada in 1992 in *R. v. Butler* through a harms-based test for obscenity. While the motivations for the two governmental rationalities (of conservatives and anti-pornography feminists) are incompatible, they seek the same results — the suppression of "obscene" pornography. Both anti-pornography feminists and conservatives share a concern for the harmful *effects* of pornography. Anti-pornography feminist scholars are concerned with the effect that pornography has on men, since pornography is eroticized violence through which men seek sexual gratification and, as a result, learn to see women as sex objects. From this perspective, obscene pornography operates at the level of preconceptions, by tainting men's thoughts and attitudes towards women (Moon 2000: 118). In addition, both groups highlight the potential for violent acts on women as a result of obscene pornography. In many cases, obscene pornography has been held by a judge to be the catalyst for the commission of a given crime. In such cases, the judge is essentially holding that the viewing of pornography is capable of corrupting morals and is presumably offending the values of the community. While some feminists argue that pornography is implicated in the commission of violent crime against women, some conservatives highlight the habituation of violence as a result of pornography only amongst the working and lower classes of men (Longino 1998: 127).

In making the case for the corrupting effects of pornography, both anti-pornography feminists and conservatives dismiss the apparent inconclusive evidence of "harm," instead drawing analogies, such as the link between smoking and cancer (Mahoney 1991: 169; Moon 2000: 265). According to Green (2000), this concept of the harms caused by obscenity also meshes quite neatly with liberal values but that "one should not be misled by the fact its most articulate defenders are feminists who say they reject liberalism, nor by the fact that many self-styled liberals reject the restrictions on freedom of expression that these feminists endorse" (Green 2000: 28). Furthermore, what Green (2000: 28) points out quite rightly is that this paradigm relies on the new and challenging claim that censorship of obscenity can promote greater liberty for all, despite the fact that "among philosophers there is still considerable debate about how best to understand the concept of harm" for the purposes of state countenancing coercion of its citizens through censorship (29).

Censorship of the kind demanded by Catherine MacKinnon (1987) and LEAF (most notably in *Butler*) exercises a familiar kind of political morality. What is missing from the paradigm of harm articulated by anti-pornography feminists is that theirs is also an expression of political morality, albeit in feminist terms. Feminists criticize conventional morality (read conservative morality) while claiming that their position is largely devoid of moral reasoning (Gotell 1997; Valverde 1999). By assuming to occupy an Archimedean point outside of discourse, anti-pornography feminists have only redefined political morality. In other words, this sort of reasoning harkens back to the *Hicklin* era, where police, prosecutors and courts were told they had to intervene to protect society from those weak-minded persons who were susceptible to the corrupting influences of pornography and other sexual vices. This notion of harm is one in which humans have little or no agency.

These examples need not suggest that anti-pornography feminists and conservatives share foundations merely because they often rely on similar arguments. However, their logic is apposite, as is their rationality for state intervention (and therefore the exercise of power). What concerns both is the prevention of constructed "harm" and the fear of that harm interfering with the social order they seek to establish. While anti-pornography feminists are concerned with the prevention of harm to society, their primary concern is for women; they posit that pornography harms women and therefore society. Similarly, conservatives are concerned primarily with harm to society; however, their primary concern is with protection of the family unit and a conservative way of life. Both may seek censorship of pornography, or at least wholesale modification of what is considered pornography, as the solution. One particular difference lies in the anti-pornography feminist claim that their position is not a moral one because of the focus on harm to women and harm to political values such as equality.

The notion of using law to promote equality is an accepted feminist legal strategy. However, the Canadian feminist debate in respect of objectionable sexual expression has pivoted between two axes. While anti-pornography feminists tend to focus on the direct and indirect harms to women as a result of pornography, anti-censorship feminists point out that criminalization has historically targeted sexual minorities. In other words, it is not the law that is a problem per se but its application by the authorities. Anti-censorship feminists would argue that *Butler* advanced "a new form of [P]uritanism, seeking to impose its values on others… [encroaching] gradually on more and more areas of people's private lives" (Easton 1994: 79). Indeed, some argue that these feminist initiatives are often more intrusive than those of conservatives in respect of pornographic expression; for instance, some radical feminists engage in more direct confrontation, such as picketing, with consumers (Easton 1994: 79). Of course, many such arguments are rejected on the basis that "feminism is constructed on a critique of the patriarchal family and society, while [P]uritanism aims at conserving the existing family structure rather than challenging it" (Easton 1994: 81). According to Koppelman, this assumption about our lack of agency is the main problem with arguments in favour of censorship advanced by conservatives and anti-pornography feminists because they

> rel[y] on the unexamined assumption that low cultural forms are devoid of complexity, and that their consumers are stupid and easily brainwashed. The dangerous fantasy at work here is a "projection of upper-class fears about lower-class men: brutish, animal-like, sexually voracious." A film is more complex than a drug, and its effects are more complex than a drug's effects. Different narratives have different meanings to different people. The state does not know enough about the consumers of pornography to intelligently censor what they get to think about, nor does it have any basis to feel confident that the readers deserve to be treated as if they were children in this way. (2008: 122–23)

In other words, the claim that obscenity is harmful rests on unexamined assumptions about human thought and actions. For Koppelman, the censorship proponents assume that human beings are not capable of resistance and self-critical capacity. Thus they seek to rely on the state to make our decisions for us.

Because the history of obscenity prosecutions has entrenched a heterosexual hegemony, anti-censorship feminists argue that censorship ought to be carefully considered and debated, in part because the dialogue about queer pornography marketed towards sexual minorities in all its explicit variants (including violence) could be justified in a liberal democracy committed to freedom and equality (Cossman et al. 1997). Like liberals, who advocate more speech rather than less speech on the grounds that evil ideas flourish under the cover of censorship, anti-censorship feminists tend to emphasize the debatable, political and identity-affirming aspects of sexual freedom (Cossman et al. 1997; Easton 1994; Johnson 1995).

Undoubtedly, the notion of equality that most feminist commentators advocate is at least apprised of the notion that women are a diverse group. Therefore, how best to achieve equality for a diverse population has been the subject of considerable debate, particularly as this question relates to the regulation of pornography. The decision of whether to allow or censor obscene expression or indecent behaviour was a hotly contested political issue in the early 1990s at the time when the obscenity law was being challenged on constitutional grounds. This debate was both academic and political because it focused on the feminist engagement with the state and because the stakes were very high for sexual minorities. At the crux of the debate was the value of promoting equality more broadly for women as a homogeneous group whilst at the same promoting sexual freedom for queer minorities. Because queer minorities have historically been subject to police harassment and criminal prosecution by the state, there was considerable concern on the part of that community about relying on liberal law to achieve sexual freedom in the name of social justice. Nevertheless, anti-censorship feminists who seek to promote the value of sexual freedom frame their political objectives in the language of liberalism (Jochelson 2009a, 2009b).

Commentators like Cossman, Bell, Gotell and Ross (1997) argue that freedom of speech furthers a number of valuable objectives: truth seeking through open debate (free speech), participation in social and political decision-making, and individual self-fulfillment and human flourishing. (Here they echo the justifications of free expression under Canadian Constitutional law — see the case of *Irwin Toy*, 1989, which said that there are three philosophies for promoting free speech.) Seating their arguments within these philosophical justifications enable anti-censorship feminists to use traditional constitutional terms as vehicles for expressing a sophisticated feminist rationality while doing an end-run around liberal law. Censoring sexually explicit materials as a means of promoting women's equality came into direct conflict with the value of sexual freedom, including the freedom to consume sexually explicit speech. Certainly, this was the issue in the *Little Sisters* case (2000) where the Supreme Court had to consider whether a queer bookshop was having its constitutional rights violated by Canada Customs policy and administrative action which resulted in the seizure of imported queer erotica at the border, but only when being imported by gay and lesbian bookstores. The consequences of the legal strategy advanced in *Butler* (i.e., the censorial potential for sexually explicit expression deemed harmful by the Court) would have a much more direct effect upon sexual minorities as well as those women who engage in the sex trade as consenting adults. These issues are explored in more detail in later chapters.

By expressing their arguments in the language of Canadian common law and in terms of the sexual actualization of the queer community, anti-censorship feminists were able to address the practical and political concerns of anti-pornography feminists, using much of the same philosophical justifications and linguistic terms that civil libertarians utilize in answering the concerns of conservatives. Such an inclination may have had the result of diluting the equality-based concerns of anti-censorship feminists, since the libertarian language allowed courts to focus on the libertarian dimensions of the argument rather than directly focusing on the equality-based concerns. This rationale was extended by the Supreme Court's decision in *Labaye*, which conceives of harm in political terms that are more abstracted than contextualized vis-à-vis so called vulnerable communities.

Cossman (1997) argued in response to the *Butler* decision that moralism continued in a modern disguise through the community standards of tolerance test. We believe that the Court's commitment to this moral discourse has been deepened and extended by the *Labaye* Court by embracing the new harm test for obscenity and indecency. We agree with Cossman (1997: 144) that "sex laws that seek to impose a conservative sexual morality, in which sex is bad — such as obscenity and the criminalization of prostitution — should be abolished" and that we can be attuned to the unique ways in which law appropriates feminist legal discourse, galvanizing negative unintended consequences for diverse sexual communities. At least part of our argument about the *Labaye* decision picks up on Gotell's (1997) analysis of the *Butler* decision, where she was able to show that "feminists have often ignored the manner in which moral ideas and rhetoric have grounded feminist speech. While purporting to embrace a politics *sans* morality, anti-pornography feminism has imbued its own assertions of feminist politics with a moral superiority, constituting its own claims about sexual representation as 'true,' as 'good,' and as the expression of the best interests of the 'disempowered'" (1997: 51).

In the main, feminist rationalities for governing sexuality see a role for the state to play in preventing or mitigating against various different conceptions or degree of social harm. These rationalities differ, however, from those typically articulated by the state (through jurisprudence delineated by the courts). The feminist governmentalities also differ from the governmentalities articulated by liberals and conservatives. For conservatives, the harm caused by obscene pornography and the unregulated sex trade is to patriarchal values. For feminists, the harm caused is to women and women's equality rights (when the state fails to intervene) or to sexual freedom for sexual minorities (when the state intervenes too much). For liberals, the harm is caused to liberalism itself (or liberal philosophical principles) when the state exercises coercive authority that violates the main principles of liberalism. However, each and every one of these discourses advance a moral claim about how to deploy governmental power through law, which in turn affects a broader social understanding of normal sexuality.

At this point in our review of the basic positions in the obscenity and indecency debate, you may be wondering what our philosophical position in the analysis is. We have, after all, summarized tomes of philosophical theory in mere pages, do we not have any philosophy of our own by which to stake a claim? We do indeed have our own brand of analytic, which we wish to apply in the context of the obscenity and indecency debate. We recognize it is a complicated approach but it also brings a new lens to an already crowded viewing field. Below we explain "our feminism," define our goals for this work and answer some theoretical concerns that might haunt both the uninitiated and more sophisticated reader. We know we find ourselves squarely in the camp of the inter-discipline, caught between the minutiae of law and the meta-analytics of sociology. We know that readers in both camps have reason to be suspicious of forging such alliances. We hope to answer those concerns below, or at least provide the reader with a case for why the approach we are taking pushes beyond the debates we have just described.

The Governmentalities of Law

Our approach is located in the broader "governmentality" literature, which builds upon the work of Foucault (1991, 1997), who developed the concept of "governmentality," or "governmental rationalities," as a way of understanding and critiquing successive forms of government or power relations. According to Rose, O'Malley and Valverde (2006: 2), for Foucault "governmentality" is in a "broad sense about the techniques and procedures for directing human behaviour. Government of children, government of souls and consciences, government of household, of a state, or of oneself" (citing Foucault 1997: 82). Using Foucaultian analytics to study judicial decisions provides us with some interesting theoretical and practical challenges from within the inter-discipline of law and sociology.

It could be argued that, as we endeavour to provide criticism of the construction of obscenity and indecency categories in law, we miss the legal point by ignoring the fundamental preoccupations of legal scholars, who locate law's significance in terms of a precedent-based system of guilt assignment and concomitant discipline. Thus, our work might seem to be of little significance to those who focus solely on the question of law enforcement because we focus on the abstract contortions used to legally manufacture obscenity and indecency (which results in punishment and has broader disciplinary effects). Those who are interested in law as precedent or law enforcement may find the analysis of the governmental rationalities underpinning law frustrating because there will be no political advocacy for law reform to promote one particular form of power move over another, such that a feminist, liberal or conservative agenda can be achieved.

Our goal is to expose the judicial packets of reasoning that together form an aspect of the governmentality of indecency and obscenity law. We seek to understand how the Canadian jurisprudence has come to attempt to control sexual expression and conduct through its justification for state intervention into the sexual lives of Canadian citizens. We understand these discursive constructions of obscenity and indecency to have broader regulatory or disciplinary effects beyond those individuals targeted for prosecution. These broader effects may even impact upon other areas of criminal law, such that the encroachments upon freedom justified through obscenity and indecency jurisprudence impact upon search and seizure or privacy laws.

This concern must not be conflated with (though it is related to) the idea of judicial creation of rules of law as the central axis of analysis. While legal tests (such as the harm test or community standards test) are interesting for their legal effect, we are interested in the way courts marshal these terms as social vacuums, which are then filled with faux objective constructs in order to render certain behaviours worthy of criminal sanction. Thus, legal tests matter for us but only as so much as they betray the socio-political machinations of the court, as refractions, reflections and sublimations of the social. In other words, the potential of law enforcement in the area, while of importance to legal scholars, is a peripheral matter to us. We study analytics, philosophy and reasoning. We are interested in the academic end of Supreme Court rationales and are less concerned about the deliverables of frontline police officers or of Statistics Canada's charging data in a given year. We are interested in concepts such as "harm," "proper functioning of society" and "morality" as opposed to more practical terms such as "appeal denied" or "sentencing hearing." While policy recommendations interest us, we believe such tangible products to be political exercises. We are happy to leave that trench work to the legal scholars who make whole careers of turning ideas into norms.

We also contest the notion that Foucault subscribed to an "expulsion thesis" (Golder and Fitzpatrick 2009: 13). The expulsion thesis is based on the notion that Foucault "failed to take proper account of law's constitutive role in society or that he offers a straightened portrait of law as a mere instrument of repression which is superseded by more productive and expansive modern modalities of power" (Golder and Fitzpatrick 2009: 13). While the turn to late modernity might not signify for proponents of the expulsion thesis the complete irrelevance of law, the use of law is seen as a "rubber stamp" on other more important forms of power (Golder and Fitzpatrick 2009: 14; Poulantzas 2000: 77). Hunt and Wickham (1994) in particular argue that the expulsion thesis is misguided. Foucault wanted us to focus our analytical concerns beyond sovereign power, which is not the same thing as abandoning law. Those who argue that law is peripheral mistakenly link all aspects of law to the power of the sovereign. This ignores the diversity of law and that law emanates from "dispersed sites of royal power, popular self regulation, customary rights, competing specialised jurisdictions… local and regional autonomies and other forms of law" (Hunt and Wickham 1994: 60).

Golder and Fitzpatrick rightly point out that by the time Foucault introduced the analytical lens of governmentality, Foucault had begun to address the intersection of law and the governance of population by noting that the relationship between "sovereignty, discipline and governmental management" is triangular (Golder and Fitzpatrick 2009: 33). In particular, this triangular relationship suggests "interrelation and co-implication of legal, disciplinary and governmental strategies" (Golder and Fitzpatrick 2009: 33; see also Rose and Valverde 1998: 542–43). On this reading, "Law is essential both to the making of 'knowledge claims' that serve to legitimize discipline and to the exercising of power on recalcitrant subjects" (Mirza 2009: 618). As such, it is important to understand that the legal categories of obscenity and indecency have broader disciplinary effects on the population than just whether the police will charge people or the Crown will be successful in its prosecutions.

One can read this shift towards understanding law as important to a governmental analysis because it recognizes a transition from law as a "blunt" instrument of the sovereign to a "tactical" administrative instrument of a governmental nature (Golder and Fitzpatrick 2009: 34). In short, law is one important aspect of our "late modern administered world" (Golder and Fitzpatrick 2009: 35). Indeed, for Golder and Fitzpatrick, law is much more than this — law is central to our current social order because it iteratively "determines the security of limits" and responds to the "disruption of those limits and their re-formation" (125). Law is not truth per se but is a "mobile and contingent" feature of the social ties that bind (Golder and Fitzpatrick 2009: 125).

The theoretical insights of Golder and Fitzpatrick ground our study of the legal rationalities (governmentalities) of obscenity and indecency law in Canada. We see the Supreme Court decisions as a reflection of governmentality that is iterative, limiting and malleable, but one that asserts a particular order, in line with the administrative ends of a late modern society. Were this a different volume, we would argue passionately and at greater length for the validity of a governmental assessment of Supreme Court analytics. For the purposes of this volume, we merely wish to give that assessment structure and leave for another day the passionate defence of the method. More importantly, we use this theoretical framework as a means of providing a critique of neoliberalism. According to Lemke (2000: 13), the strength in this approach "consists in the fact that it construes neo-liberalism… above all as a political project that endeavors to create a social reality that it suggests already exists."

When we use the governmentality framework to understand neoliberalism as a political project (or projects), it is possible to take account of the different ways in which the courts render their knowledge of society as "real" and to take into account the possible consequences of these "truths" (Lemke 2000: 14). By examining the "truth effects" that are produced when the Court justifies state power to protect society from the dangers of obscenity or indecency, we are able to bring into sharper focus the relationships of power between the state and the individual, but also amongst individuals and themselves. The issue we confront with respect to the legal rationalities underpinning criminalization of obscenity and bawdy houses strikes at what Dean (1999) characterizes as the central responsibility of the state in a liberal regime. The "state's responsibility is to protect this freedom, by refraining from intervention in the spheres of social life considered 'private,' such as the family and the market, without good reason" (Harris 2006: 1562, citing Dean 1999).

Rather than positioning normative outcomes for women as the pivot point of analysis, we shift focus to examine the kind of work constitutional values "do and ask": How does constitutional rule itself govern through liberal values like freedom and equality? While some have regarded descriptions of the logic that underpins justifications for power as apolitical, only part of the overall theoretical approach is descriptive. Governmentality studies provide an important point of dialogue in informing the activist project. Indeed the practice of *critique* offered by governmentality studies provides an opportunity to rethink and problematize the *effects* of activist political strategies which mobilize state power. Because these offer suggestions for particular outcomes for women and sexual minorities in the context of obscenity law, it is important to understand the logic that underpins their justifications for state intervention and punishment.

Rather than advocating for a particular outcome in line with a particular social justice program (such as using the obscenity law to promote women's equality, or preventing the state from discriminating against gay and lesbian sexually explicit materials through seizure by Canada Border Services), our aim is to provide an analytic of government. Thus, we see a utility in the dialogic nature of description without arguing for a particular outcome or foundation (Fish 2008). In the case of obscenity and indecency law, the techniques and rationalities underpinning regulation are given content, in part, by a reading of judicial text. Thus, we see case law as not merely treatises of precedent but as reflections and refractions of societal ordering. Put otherwise, we view case law as a norm of the social, not just as a norm of the rule (Golder and Fitzpatrick 2009: 124–30).

In our forthcoming chapters then, we see an analytic rooted in governmentality, which is unlike moral-conservative, liberal or feminist perspectives, because the approach is not rooted in any particular foundational claims. Our sole foundation rests upon understanding the nature of techniques of governmentality, such as harm- and risk-based legal tests. The feminist and queer discourses preceding us, in the context of obscenity and indecency law, have been interested in disposition and effect on disparate communities. They have sought to destabilize conservative morality through re-interpretation of legal tests for obscenity and as a means of achieving political change. The change advocated has on occasion resulted in controversial results within feminist and queer communities. One need only read the ensuing scholarship after *Butler* and *Little Sisters* to confirm this conclusion. We too are interested in the outcome of these cases (disposition) but also wish to examine rationalities for state intervention (legal discourse). Here, we study in depth what each line of decision-making might reveal about the rationales behind governmental techniques. This approach may reveal the tools and objectives behind the legal means through which we regulate our sexuality in the exercise of state power. As Dean argues, we wish to undertake a form of criticism which "seeks to make explicit the thought that, while often taking a material form, is largely tacit in the way in which we govern and are governed and in the language, practices and techniques by which we do so" (1999: 36). We may thus uncover deviations or similarities with past legal practice. Hence, we are less interested in the explosion of hidden meanings than describing the power effects of those meanings. Based on our findings, we will be happy to leave those with activist foundations to achieve whatever goals they wish. When they are done we would be pleased to then problematize their analytic and start the process afresh.

The embrace of political morality and unruly sexuality by government may be desirable, deleterious or benign. While the Court has sought out reasonable and objective standards of proof through its various iterations of the meanings of obscenity and indecency, we are interested in observing the contextualized subjectivities that informed the Court's attempts to articulate universal standards of corruption, community and harm (each used as a barometer of obscenity or indecency throughout Canadian history). We approach this endeavour agnostically, with some scepticism as to whether an objective definition of indecency or obscenity is even possible.

In our forthcoming chapters, then, we examine the *Labaye* decision, placing it in its jurisprudential history. We unpack the rationales that inform the judicial decisions to understand the rules of the social that the Court creates. We place these rules in their iterative place, understanding that common law operationalizes law but more importantly creates meaning and influences societal ordering. This has an impact on how we govern our sexual selves. The analysis helps us understand the way justices of the Supreme Court operationalize and create a "properly functioning society" and the place of sexually explicit materials in that society. The analysis also reveals the way sexual subjects govern themselves in response to the judicial prose. This is a new project of judicial analytics. We imagine the project as a practice of justice.

Notes

1. Pornography has many different meanings depending upon one's political perspective. When academics and jurists speak of "pornography," they generally are speaking of expressive descriptions and/or depictions that involve, in large measure, individuals engaging in explicit (and often graphic) sexual acts and the concomitant surrounding context. The key divide in respect of a definition of obscenity is between those who argue for its censorship because it causes moral harm (Benedet 2001) and those who argue that its censorship cuts off critical analyses of the messages it sometimes endorses about human sexuality (Koppelman 2005, 2006, 2008).
2. "Common bawdy house" is the legal term used to describe private spaces in which sex is exchanged for money. In the *Criminal Code*, under section 210, a bawdy house is merely "a place that is kept or occupied, or resorted to by one or more persons, for the purpose of prostitution or the practice of acts of indecency."
3. *Butler* was the internationally recognized Canadian Supreme Court decision which first considered whether the anti-obscenity law contained in the *Criminal Code* violated the freedom of expression guarantee under the *Charter*.
4. By functionalism, we mean "the effort to impute, as rigorously as possible, to each feature, custom, or practice, its effect on the functioning of a supposedly stable, cohesive system" (Bourricaud 1981: 94).
5. Angela P. Harris (2006) advances this argument in relation to recent United States case law dealing with same-sex marriage, but especially *R. v. Lawrence* (2006).
6. This is the precise issue to be considered by the Quebec Court in the Couture matter.
7. Written by Vladimir Nabokov, *Lolita* (1955) chronicles the sexual obsession a middle-aged man has for a twelve-year-old girl.
8. Interestingly, this is the very point acceded to by McLachlan J. (as she was then), in the *Keegstra* decision (1990), where, in her dissenting opinion, she argued for more speech rather than less. The dissenting judges were concerned that censorship of evil ideas would dull the political speech of all Canadians and render obsolete the corner soapbox. Ironically, the protection of speech is abandoned by McLachlan J. in *R. v. Butler*, when she argued that the corner soapbox was closed for pornography.
9. The Canadian Civil Liberties Association (CCLA) is a "national organization that was constituted in 1964 to promote respect for and observance of fundamental human rights and civil liberties. Our work, which includes research, public education and advocacy aims to defend and ensure the protection and full exercise of those rights and liberties" <ccla.org/about-us/overview/>.
10. According to its website, "LEAF — the Women's Legal Education and Action

Fund — is a national charitable organization that works toward ensuring the law guarantees substantive equality for all women in Canada. Its mandate is to ensure the rights of women and girls in Canada, as guaranteed in the Canadian Charter of Rights and Freedoms, are upheld in our courts, human rights commissions and government agencies and take actions to reveal how factors such as race, class, Aboriginal status, sexual orientation, ability, and religion compound discrimination against women <www.leaf.ca/about/index. html#target>.

11. Group Against Pornography (GAP) notes that it "is a grassroots, non-profit, volunteer organization, founded in 1988 to combat the proliferation of hardcore obscene pornography in Canada. GAP believes pornography plays an accessory role in negative social issues such as sexual child abuse, violence against women, date rape, inequality, relationship and family breakdown, youth crime, promiscuity, sexually transmitted disease" <www.wildfeatherfree.blogspot. com/2007/01/group-against-pornography.html>.

12. Canadian Council of Muslim Women (CCMW) "is a national organization with chapters across the country. CCMW believes that Muslim women must develop their Muslim identity while being a part of and making a positive contribution to Canadian society, and that they must provide positive role models for Muslim youth" <ccmw.com/about_ccmw.html>.

Chapter Two

Political Morality from *Hicklin* to *Butler* and *Little Sisters*

In this chapter, we explain how Canadian obscenity law, which governs sexually explicit obscene materials, has developed since the mid-nineteenth century. This chapter illustrates how common law justifications for criminalizing sexually explicit "obscene" and materials have always affirmed a particular kind of liberal notion that state coercion is justified only in relation to harm. What is important to note however, is that since Confederation, the Canadian courts have conceptualized the social harms of obscenity and indecency in relation to the proper functioning of society. In the sociological sense, functionalist views of society rest on the idea that societies are homeostatic, in that they strive to maintain equilibrium in the face of practices that undermine balance. Equilibrium is achieved in part through socialization of citizens to adopt society's basic values and norms in order to maintain a societal consensus. Where the socialization process breaks down and fails to produce conformity, social control mechanisms — such as criminal law — step in to provide correction by restoring conformity or punishing non-conforming members of society. This Durkheimian world view, in which "society is independent of the individuals that it moulds and shapes" (Pavlich 2011: 73), is the one largely adopted by the Canadian courts in adjudicating both obscenity and indecency cases.

The Canadian courts have consistently justified the criminalization of "obscenity," constituting it as harm to the proper functioning of society. The rationale for criminalizing works as "obscene" has been justified in relation to the policing of moral values to promote social cohesion. This functionalist view of society and the role of law in maintaining social order has enabled the courts to justify both policing obscenity and upholding the obscenity provision of the *Criminal Code*. The courts see their role as promoting societal equilibrium that is thrown off balance by the circulation, distribution and consumption of "obscene" materials. The pages that follow show that this sociological functionalism can wear many political masks.

Obscenity cases leading up to the Supreme Court of Canada's decision in *R. v. Butler* can be divided into two distinct categories: the *Hicklin* era (1868–1962) followed by the community standards era (1962–1992). During these two periods, the common law language of "obscenity" shifted from one rooted in concerns about the so-called "dangerous" and working classes to one allowing certain sexuality explicit materials to circulate so long as they are tolerated by the community. Community standards of tolerance were determined by judges, who could sometimes rely on relatively ambiguous evidence of societal harm.

The *Hicklin* Era (1868–1962)

By the mid-nineteenth century, the state's criminalization of sexuality was firmly linked to its efforts at repressing popular use of sexual imagery in all sorts of political and social expression. The widespread availability of sexually explicit imagery and text that followed the industrial revolution caused a "moral panic" about the social harm that would result from the mass consumption of pornography (Johnson 1995). Victorian attitudes towards sexuality supported the claim that pornography was a vice that would cause all sorts of social ills, including sex crime, should it fall into the hands of the working or "dangerous classes," whose minds were seen as easily susceptible to corruption. If allowed to circulate freely, pornography would threaten the stability of society, and its criminalization was justified in relation to maintaining social order.

The earliest common law definition of "obscenity" in both Anglo-Canadian and Anglo-American law was established in the 1868 English case *R. v. Hicklin* (Koppelman 2006: 66). The court's decision in *Hicklin* (1868) was concerned with the corruption of morals, particularly among the "weak minded." The concern was not for members of the upper class who might take possession of obscene materials, but rather it was an attempt to regulate the "dangerous classes": the lower classes, men, the young and the uneducated — that is, those who were constitutionally unable to resist the sexually explicit material's influences (Cossman et al. 1997: 12; Johnson 1995: 43–45). The test asked "whether the tendency of the matter charged as obscenity is to deprave and corrupt those whose minds are open to such immoral influences and into whose hands the publication of this sort is likely to fall." (*Hicklin* 1868: 373). Criminal regulation was thus justified on the paternalistic grounds of both individual and societal protection from harm. Pornography was seen as a vice that needed to be controlled, like drugs or alcohol, because consumption by the "morally inferior" lower classes would endanger the proper functioning of society (295). This reading of obscenity would protect the "nuclear" family unit, reduce criminality among the "dangerous classes" and preserve an assumed moral order (295). In practice, obscenity laws were concerned with policing sexual morality and degeneracy and controlling sex outside of marriage (McLaren and McLaren 1986; Valverde 1991).

Following the adoption of the *Criminal Code* in 1892, only five Canadian obscenity cases were reported between 1900 and 1940 — all of which followed the *Hicklin* precedent (Johnson 1999: 294). Materials that educated consumers about fertility control — or ways to bring about the menstrual flow — were the subject of prosecution under the obscenity statute because they were sexual in nature and seen as "tend[ing] to corrupt morals," which the law prohibited as a means of promoting the heterosexual monogamous family form. In 1877, Charles Bradlaugh and Annie Besant had been prosecuted in England under the obscenity statute for disseminating contraceptive information when they republished a forty-year-old text called *Fruits of Philosophy* by Charles Knowlton (Peart and Levy 2008: 345). According to Peart and Levy, the debate at trial centred around whether contraceptive information ought to be widely disseminated. John Stuart Mill made the case for wide dissemination of the information, against Charles Darwin, who argued that it should only be available to the rich or through a physician (Peart and Levy 2008: 344). The trial jury found Bradlaugh and Besant guilty for publishing obscene materials, but the decision was reversed on appeal (345).

Between 1944 and 1959 in Canada, there were some changes made to the *Hicklin* test in common law. In 1944, the addition of *mens rea* meant that, for a successful prosecution, producers, distributors and sellers were required to possess criminal intent (*Conway v. The King* [1944]). And, in 1953, the Court considered which part of the population was susceptible to corrupting influences (*R. v. National News*). In 1954, the Court introduced the notion of a contemporary standard for judging obscenity because materials that "deprave and corrupt" one generation may not do so to the next. The Court also demanded that sexually explicit materials be judged in their entirety to allow for works of literary merit (*R. v. Martin Secker Warburg Ltd. And Others*). By 1959, following recommendations from a special committee of the Senate chaired by E.D. Fulton in 1952, the statute was revised so as to define "obscenity" as "any publication a dominant characteristic of which is the undue exploitation of sex, and any one or more of the following subjects, namely, crime, horror, cruelty and violence shall be deemed to be obscene" (now s. 163 of the *Criminal Code of Canada*). With this revision we see the abandonment of Parliament's attempts to control sexuality as an immoral or wicked habit and the introduction of the political value of inoculating society against violence when coupled with the sex. What amounts to the "undue exploitation" of sex would eventually become a standard for the community to determine, but in practice judges would perform that work.

The Community Standards Era (1962–1992)

For thirty years, between 1962 and 1992, the courts developed the common law on obscenity doctrine. For the most part, when adjudicating cases that came before them, the judiciary focused upon the nature and role of the community in determining standards of tolerance for undue exploitation of sex. Their focus was less on the impact of pornography on women and women's equality but rather on determining that which went beyond the limits of permissive explicit sexual expression. Thus were the limits determined by the society, which was, in turn, given content by the term "community."

With the shift towards the language of community standards we see paternalistic moralism operationalized in law. The notion that judges could act as arbiters of community standards meant that the law could force consumers and producers of pornography to be *better people* by criminalizing pornography (Green 2000: 27). The use of community standards was constructed by the courts as means of creating some sort of objective test by which to give "obscenity" meaning. The struggle for objectivity is still one which plagues the courts (Jochelson 2009a, 2009b).

In *R. v. Brodie* [1962], shortly after the enactment of what is now s. 163(8) of the *Criminal Code*, the Supreme Court introduced the community standards test in the prosecution of D.H. Lawrence's classic of English literature *Lady Chatterley's Lover*. The test for obscenity was redefined to determine whether the *dominant characteristic* of the material was the *undue exploitation* of sex; the application of this test required that the work be read as a whole in order to determine its dominant purpose (*R. v. Brodie* 1962: 702). Judson J. noted that *community standards* were relevant in deeming whether undue exploitation of sex had occurred since a community had tangible views of decency, cleanliness and dirtiness (*R. v. Brodie* 1962: 705). Whereas the *Hicklin* Court authorized the upper classes to proscribe access to sexually explicit materials on the basis of their own moral judgment of others' corruptibility, the discourse of the *Brodie* Court allowed the community as a whole to participate in the determination of harm. In practice, this work was done by judges. For Judson J., if the dominant purpose of the speech in question was the undue exploitation of sex, then the material contravened the legislation on the grounds that the community would not tolerate undue exploitation of sex, or "harm." However, if the dominant purpose of the material was not the undue exploitation of sex, the material was acceptable and therefore not harmful (*R. v. Brodie* 1962: 702). The obscenity paradigm adopted into law was one that enabled judges to speak for the majority on the question of virtue versus vice: harmless versus harmful. Moreover, it empowered the judiciary to limit free expression on the basis of whether or not the courts (speaking on behalf of society) determined the exploitation of sex to be "undue." The old language of the *Hicklin* era had become obsolete, replaced with new language of community standards of tolerance test to determine undue exploitation of sex. In determining what was harmful, the Court considered that harm caused to any one member of society caused harm to society as a whole. In this sense, the Court did not abandon the logic of the *Hicklin* era, with its view of society as an organism. Where one part was affected, the whole was affected, requiring judicial authority to protect the whole organism.

The juridical harm test for obscenity was further developed in *R. v. Dominion News and Gifts* [1964]. Here, the Court affirmed Freedman J.A.'s dissent in the Manitoba Court of Appeal, which noted that community standards should be an average of the community's thinking — somewhere between the base and the puritan (*R. v. Dominion* 1964: 251; *R. v. Dominion* 1963: 116). This could avoid a "subjective approach, with the result dependent upon, and varying with, the personal tastes and predilections of the particular Judge who happens to be trying the case" (*R. v. Dominion* 1963: 116). Using this test, the Court surmised that the extremes of Canadian viewpoints would play a small role in assessing community values, as a mainstream consensus emerged. Here we see the judiciary's first attempts at establishing an "objective" test for undue exploitation causing harm to society, by formally distancing the test from the individual predilections of judges or what could be perceived as deeply patriarchal or heterosexist community values.

Further revision of the test occurred in *R. v. Towne Cinema Theatres Ltd.* [1985]. There, Dickson C.J. introduced again the notion of "objectivity" to the legal exercise of determining contemporary Canadian community standards, to avoid projecting "one's own personal ideas of what is tolerable" (*R. v. Towne Cinema Theatres Ltd.* 1985: para. 33). This so-called objective test was supposed to be one of *tolerance* rather than *taste* and concerned itself with what Canadians would tolerate *other* Canadians seeing (para. 34, emphasis added). In other words, we shift perspective slightly to view sexually explicit materials not from our own likes or dislikes, but to ask the question: What kind of sexually explicit materials would the community tolerate *other* Canadians consuming? One particular difficulty remained, in that the judge, rather than using *evidence* of Canadian attitudes, might instead infer the standard from her or his knowledge of those attitudes. Nevertheless, the concept of "undue exploitation" shifted. Sex was exploitative when it was coupled with, for instance, violence; a liberal harms-based test of obscenity was emerging (Johnson 1999: 296).

The terms "corruption" and "degradation of morals" were being transformed into more concrete liberal legal language — in practice, "judges, customs agents, and police would deliver the united concepts of undue exploitation that violate community standards to justify... [regulation]... that failed to conform to their individual notions of decency" (Johnson 1999: 297). Feminists would later criticize the community standard test for undue exploitation on the grounds that homophobic and/or morally conservative judges would insert their own values for community values and find gay and lesbian sexually explicit materials to be obscene or indecent.

The Post-Charter Community Standards of Tolerance for Harm Era (*R. v. Butler* [1992])

The Winnipeg police charged Donald Victor Butler, the owner of Avenue Video Boutique on Main Street, under section 163 (then section 159) of the *Criminal Code*, with possession and distribution of obscenity. Founded in 1987, the store dealt in pornographic videos and magazines as well as sexual paraphernalia. Soon after the store's opening, the police, with a search warrant in hand, confiscated incriminating property. In the fall of that same year, after the confiscation, Butler restarted the business at the same location and the police almost immediately arrested Butler and an employee. Over seventy charges of obscenity-based offences were lobbed at the pair. Butler and his employee were found guilty on a small number of the charges (eight and two respectively) and had to pay fines of $1000 per offence.

The case drew unparalleled attention from public interest groups because it was the first to challenge the obscenity law under the newly passed *Charter of Rights and Freedoms*. Many of these groups would eventually intervene in the legal proceedings to bring their political perspectives to court. The intervention of LEAF and the British Columbia Civil Liberties Association (BCCLA)[1] are perhaps most salient as they illustrate the profound disagreements that non-litigants brought to the debate about pornography aimed at the heterosexual marketplace.

Intervener Disputes in Butler

Ultimately, the Court's recognition that "obscenity" causes harm[2] to the political notion of equality arose partly from LEAF's arguments in favour of upholding the obscenity statute despite its potential interference with the guarantee to freedom of expression. As a contemporary feminist advocacy group, LEAF's arguments for legal intervention were rooted in a commitment to improving women's social status through law. In response to the *Charter* challenge, LEAF responded with a Section 15 equality argument in favour of retaining the obscenity clause of the *Criminal Code*. Their harms-based equality approach to pornography clashed with the civil libertarian approach, which privileged freedom of expression over equality (as embodied by the BCCLA). LEAF's legal team sought to have obscenity defined as a practice of sex discrimination that harms women's equality. Unlike the Court, LEAF viewed inequality as a systemic feature of society and sought to use the law to promote women's equality through the criminalization of violent, degrading and dehumanizing pornography. LEAF's position was informed by the arguments that had been made in the U.S. context by Catherine MacKinnon and Andrea Dworkin. LEAF and other feminists argued that pornography ought not to be protected speech because it causes harm to women. Busby (1993: 1) argued that the *Charter's* freedom of expression guarantee ought to be interpreted against the backdrop of the *Charter's* equality guarantee, with harm to women being the focal point. LEAF's argument, outlined in their *Factum of the Intervener*, submitted to the Supreme Court of Canada, was that pornography is a form of sex discrimination that affects individual women and women as a group and that society's social interest in equality outweighs any protection to free expression guaranteed under section 2(b) of the *Charter*. LEAF submitted that some pornography in both its violent and degrading forms ought not to have *Charter* protection under section 2(b). LEAF argued that society had an interest in regulating pornography through criminal law using a harms-based equality approach that would allow infringement upon free expression. According to LEAF, the societal interest in equality outweighs the societal interest in protecting violent and degrading forms of sexually explicit expression. LEAF's position rested on the notion that violent, degrading and dehumanizing pornography causes actual harm to women in its production and attitudinal harm to women as a group because it changes how women are viewed in society.

LEAF advanced the argument that the Court ought to revise the community standards test by anchoring it in a more harms-based principle, moving away from grounding the test on explicitness (LEAF Factum *Butler* 1991: 5). LEAF noted that from the early 1980s onwards, the courts had been relying upon the notion of the harms of pornography to interpret its content rather than the sexually explicit nature of the materials (LEAF Factum *Butler* 1991: 6). In cases such as *R. v. Wagner* (1985) and *R. v. Red Hot Video* (1985), the lower courts continued to focus on social harm and threats to society from the attitudinal changes that ostensibly result from exposure to violent, degrading and dehumanizing pornography as the justification for its continued criminalization. The Supreme Court confirmed this line of reasoning in *Towne Cinema Theatres Ltd. v. The Queen* [1985] when it found that the Court had the obligation to determine whether the materials in question amounted to the "undue" exploitation of sex. The community standards of tolerance test to determine undue exploitation rested on the notion that the judge would determine the community consensus in order to inoculate society as a whole from the harm caused by obscenity — society would not tolerate "undue" exploitation of sex because it caused harm. LEAF read this decision as in line with the protection and promotion of women's equality, despite the Court's more general language. LEAF's legal team members believed that the Court would be *promoting* equality in a society characterized by inequality between the sexes, by criminalizing obscenity.

The seemingly more liberal test would placate the anti-pornography feminists by enabling the state to continue to prosecute on the grounds that attitudinal harm interferes with women's equality. In fact, in the year following the *Butler* decision, MacKinnon, who aided LEAF in the drafting of the factum, published a book called *Only Words*, where she argued: "If the community standards applied were interpreted to prohibit harm to women as harm to the community, it was constitutional because it promoted sex equality" (MacKinnon 1993: 101). In other words, the feminist analysis of the community standards of tolerance test meshed quite nicely with the functionalist jurisprudence that had already been in place since the early twentieth century. Indeed, very shortly after the decision was rendered, Cossman argued quite correctly that the decision is a subtle joining of the anti-pornography feminist equality claims with the courts' traditional moral conservative approach to harm (Cossman et al. 1997). The pro-censorship argument of the anti-pornography feminists in favour of retaining the obscenity provision on the grounds that the state's role is to promote equality rested on the liberal notion that harm to society (understood as harm to women's equality) justifies criminal sanction.

However, this position was not supported by all in the Canadian feminist community. Socialist feminists and sex radicals were more concerned about the effects of criminal regulation on sexual freedom than the theoretical harms caused by obscene materials. The anti-censorship feminists pointed to the role of the law in criminalizing marginalized sexuality to promote a hetero-normative sexuality (see, for example, Burstyn 1985; Cossman et al. 1997; Johnson 1995; Lacombe 1994; Segal and McIntosh 1993).

The arguments of LEAF were rebutted by the intervener BCCLA, which embodied a view that was highly critical of LEAF's contentions. Their factum contained a strong assertion of the value of sexual expression in a democratic community. The factum drew on the argument that pornography can contain meaningful content. In the BCCLA's view, sexual norms, behaviours and identities have a strong influence on the structure of political life: "Sexual expression tells us something about ourselves that some of us, at least, prefer not to know. It threatens to explode the uneasy accommodation between sexual impulse and social custom — to destroy the carefully spun web holding sexuality in place" (BCCLA Factum *Butler* 1991: 4). The BCCLA also emphasized that sexually explicit expression was of particular importance to certain groups within the community; for instance, for gays and lesbians, sexual speech is a means of "self-affirmation" in "a generally hostile world" (6). The use of pornography made by and for sexual minorities provided a mechanism by which sexual minorities feel that their sexual orientation is valid due to the mere availability of such pornographic works; if these works are censored, such restriction countenances the view that queerness is less worthy of protection than the heterosexual lifestyle. This results in a view of sexuality that is antithetical to the guarantees of the *Charter* towards equality. Further, the availability of such works challenges conventional majoritarian norms and over time leads to gradual acceptance of queerness in the mainstream.

Pornography, according to the BCCLA, has many different meanings. Pornography can endorse male power and countenance misogyny. However, pornography can also flout conventional sexual mores, ridicule sexual hypocrisy, underscore the importance of sexual norms and support the notion of sex for pleasure (BCCLA Factum *Butler* 1991: 5). Therefore, for the BCCLA, the impact of pornography was not linear or straightforward but was rather "multiple, layered, and highly contextual" (BCCLA Factum *Butler* 1991: 11).

The BCCLA was also concerned that the community standards test proposed in *Butler* would impose judicial views of "correct" sexuality on a diverse community (BCCLA Factum *Butler* 1991: 15; Cossman et al. 1997: 77). Indeed, the impact of the test would be to favour those views that are closest to the majoritarian beliefs about appropriate sexuality; this would discriminate against queerness because the sexual norms of the queer community by definition are non-majoritarian (BCCLA Factum *Butler* 1991: 5; Cossman et al. 1997: 77). In this respect, both the feminist anti-censorship rationalities meshed with those of liberals interested in promoting sexual freedom.

The Decision

Butler would unsuccessfully allege at the Supreme Court of Canada that his freedom of expression was unjustifiably infringed by the obscenity provisions of the *Criminal Code*. While notably, the Court did find that sexually explicit expression was speech under the *Charter*, they found that the law was a reasonable limit in Canadian society and was therefore not unconstitutional. The law was a justifiable infringement of the freedom of expression of the aggrieved video storeowner. The common law community standards test was re-deployed in *Butler*, the first Supreme Court case to formulate the community standards of tolerance approach under the *Charter* in the context of a constitutional challenge to the obscenity provision.

The *Butler* Court significantly clarified the common law definition of obscenity for the purposes of criminal liability. Sopinka J. set out a three-tiered test for determining which materials would fail the community standards of tolerance test for undue exploitation/harm, which flowed from the Court's interpretation of the pre-*Charter* case law. The three tiers were: (1) explicit sex with violence; (2) explicit sex without violence but which subjects people to treatment that is degrading and dehumanizing; and (3) explicit sex without violence that is neither degrading nor dehumanizing that does not involve children (*R. v. Butler* 1992: 484). The grounds set out by the Court for criminal liability are firmly linked to harm, and the risk of harm, to the proper functioning of society. According to Sopinka J., the community would not tolerate others being exposed to the undue exploitation of sex, defined as sex coupled with violence and, when a risk exists, sex that is not necessarily coupled with violence but is nonetheless degrading and dehumanizing (*R. v. Butler* 1992: 485). Tier one would always fail the community standards test due to the pairing of sex and violence, while tier two might fail the test if the risk of harm was substantial, i.e., when the undue exploitation of sex could lead to anti-social attitudes and behaviour. Tier three would not fail the test and is therefore not indecency. Both of the first two violations of community standards were linked to the individual (attitudinal harm) and to social cohesion (harm to the proper functioning of society). No longer seen in terms of offence to morals, the community standards became the new test with neoliberal political morality replacing conservative religious morality as the justification for criminalization. The logic the courts rely upon is the same, but the language invoked to operationalize censorship is different.

Ultimately, the courts are concerned with society as a whole rather than promoting women's equality per se. It is only insofar as society's interest in proper functioning is concerned that women's right to equality is considered relevant to obscenity determinations. The community standards of tolerance test for "undueness" continues to assume a consensual moral order. According to the *Butler* Court's post-*Charter* rationale, the impact of obscenity on society leads to abuse, harm and risk of harm (to both women and men as individuals), which interferes with the proper functioning of society. Criminalization is therefore justified, but equality becomes but one element of a proper functioning society.

It is presumed that society exists in a state of equilibrium, which includes equality, but that the existence of "obscenity" throws that stability off balance. In relation to social cohesion, harm to equality resulting from exposure to violent and degrading pornography was flagged as one element justifying state action that infringes upon freedom of expression. The Court's main agreement with LEAF's argument is found in its acceptance of the idea that violent sexually explicit expression would, and that degrading and dehumanizing pornography could, result in harm to society by causing attitudinal changes, principally, in men.

R. v. Butler extended *R. v. Brodie* to include specific kinds of pornography that will be deemed criminal, which satisfied the anti-pornography feminist critics, who oppose the sexual objectification of women in its violent and degrading forms. According to the *Butler* Court, "obscene" pornography is that which the Canadian community would *not* tolerate others being exposed to on the basis of the degree of harm that would flow from such exposure. The Court's argument was that the community would not tolerate the undue exploitation of sex, because such exploitation caused harm to the participants and to men and women more broadly as citizens of a liberal democracy who ought to be protected from such harm. Harm in this context ran a broad spectrum from harm to those who participate in making pornography to the harms of degradation and dehumanization that may inure from the promulgation of pornography throughout society. Most notably, the Court recognized that harm could include harms to equality — a s. 15 guarantee under the *Charter* (*R. v. Butler* 1992: 479).

Homophobic Discretion after *Butler*

Following *Butler*, the anti-pornography feminist scholars were enthused as to the decision's implications. Andrea Dworkin noted: "The *Butler* decision is probably the best articulation of how pornography, and what kinds of pornography, hurt the civil status of women" (Strossen 1995: 228). Catherine MacKinnon noted that *Butler* was "a stunning victory for women. This is of world historic importance. This makes Canada the first place in the world that says what is obscene is what harms women, not what offends our values" (Strossen 1995: 228). However, within the first three years after *Butler*, over half of all Canadian feminist bookstores were victims of customs' confiscation or detention (Strossen 1995: 231).

The results following *Butler* were sharply focused on the gay and lesbian community and its works. One of the first acts of Toronto police was to raid Glad Day Bookshop and to confiscate the lesbian erotic magazine, *Bad Attitude*. Perhaps most striking is that the publication at the time sold only forty copies every two months in Canada; even LEAF admitted that the publication was "hardly a threat to women's equality" (Strossen 1995: 232). Nadine Strossen notes that while Glad Day's owner and manager were arrested for selling *Bad Attitude*, a nearby mainstream bookstore that also sold it was left undisturbed (232).

In the case brought against Glad Day Bookshop's principals,[3] at issue was a story entitled "Wunna my Fantasies," a sadomasochistic lesbian work in which an unwitting participant eventually succumbs and enjoys submitting to forced masturbation (otherwise known as a "mock rape" scene). Following the newly established *Butler* test, Paris J., found the story degrading to women, despite the ultimate consent of the women in the story; further, he dismissed the fact the aggressor in the story was female as irrelevant, noting that the community standards of tolerance test was blind to sexual orientation or practices. Any considerations given to the sexual orientation would constitute an unwarranted application of the test. Paris J., noted that if one replaced the aggressor in this article with a man "there would be very few people in the community who would not recognize the potential for harm" (*R. v. Scythes* 1993: 5). Here we see an immediate example of the way in which the harm test is operationalized to target lesbian sado-masochism pornography. On a narrow reading of the case, the Court finds harm in the coupling of sex and violence regardless of sexual orientation. However, the fact that there are thousands of similar portrayals of sex coupled with violence in heterosexual materials that are never prosecuted illustrates the discriminatory use of the obscenity law to target queer pornography.

In a second case brought against Glad Day Bookshop, all of the gay publications that were seized were held to be "degrading and dehumanizing" under the *Butler* harm standard. The court noted that the gay publications showed no apparent real and meaningful human relationship (*R. v. Glad Day* 1992). This Hicklinesque reasoning was later clarified in a different case in which the Ontario Court of Appeal noted that failure to portray meaningful relationships did not result in a work being obscene (*R. v. Ronish* 1993: 82). In other words, sexually explicit materials could depict what some might consider to be "amoral" sexual conduct without being subject to criminal sanction.

In addition, following *Butler*, other adverse effects on the gay and lesbian publishing community have been documented. According to Strossen, the largest exporter of gay and lesbian literature to Canada had 73 percent of its shipments detained in spring 1993 (1995: 234). Indeed, the *Globe and Mail* estimated that 75 percent of shipments to gay and lesbian bookstores were opened, delayed, lost, forgotten and sent back (235).[4] Ultimately, LEAF, the intervener who advanced that anti-pornography feminist stance in *Butler*, met with anti-censorship activists and issued a joint news release that "unanimously condemned the use of the *Butler* decision to justify the discriminatory use of law to harass and intimidate lesbians and gays and sex trade workers" (Strossen 1995: 241).[5] Through these cases and the subsequent law enforcement responses after *Butler*, we see the law attempting to protect society from harmful sexually explicit materials while meeting the equality requirement of the *Charter*. Both straight and queer communities are prohibited from selling, distributing and consuming sexually explicit materials that couple sex and violence under the new *Butler* test because sex and violence are not tolerated under the community standards test because it causes harm to society. The legal regime creates a society that will tolerate the inclusion of gays and lesbians on grounds of political rights, but it will not tolerate any sexual habits that are not tolerated for heterosexuals. Perfect formal equality is therefore rendered through obscenity law in order to preserve the proper functioning of society and protect us from harm.

By grounding the test for censorship in societal harm, the Supreme Court continues to rationalize censorship of sexually explicit materials in the paternalistic terms (Koppelman 2005). When it created a distinction between sexually explicit popular cultural materials (mainstream pornography) and sexually explicit fine literature (*Lady Chatterley's Lover*), the

Court was able to extend the *Hicklin* era test in liberal rather than overtly conservative language.

In practice, the liberal internal necessities test and the community standards of tolerance test to determine undue exploitation of sex laid out in *R. v. Brodie* provided the justification for the criminal regulation of mass-produced pornography consumed largely amongst working-class men. The concern was not for the effects of such materials on the upper-class men, who may consume mass-produced pornography along with fine literature such as *Lady Chatterley's Lover*, but with the effects it has on "attitudes" of those who consume only the mass-produced low-brow works and how those attitudes would in turn affect the functioning of society. In purporting to provide a legal-positivist test for determining harm to society to justify censorship, the twentieth-century courts, up to and including the *Butler* era, are no different in their logic from the nineteenth-century courts, concerned with societal harms caused to those whose minds are susceptible to corrupting influences; the concern remains attitudinal and is linked to societal functioning. With the *Butler* decision, we see this logic extended to include a justification for societal protection based on the notion that it causes harm to consumers of obscenity, which in turn ostensibly harms equality as a political and moral value which would interfere with society's proper functioning.

Butler's Lil Sista: The Little Sisters Case

In this section we discuss the Supreme Court of Canada adjudication of the *Little Sisters* case, which provided an opportunity for the Court to revisit the *Butler* community standards of tolerance approach to the harms of obscenity, in the context of queer pornographies. Different feminist arguments would be placed before the Court, and ultimately, the Court would uphold a modified *Butler* standard. The Court would clarify its functionalist commitments by making it clear that the *Butler* approach was intended to protect all members of society from the harms of obscenity rather than simply the equality interests of women or minority sex groups.

Little Sisters Book and Art Emporium began fighting Canada Customs in 1986 for routinely seizing materials imported from the United States under Canada's obscenity law. The majority of the bookstore's products were imported from the United States. Since 1985, many books and magazines purchased by Little Sisters had been seized, detained, prohibited or destroyed by customs officials acting under customs legislation. Many of these same materials were available at mainstream Canadian bookstores, so it was clear that Canada Customs was targeting only the gay and lesbian bookstores in Canada. According to bookstore co-owner Jim Deva:

> We decided to begin with the most blatant example of censorship

and challenged Customs' seizure of an issue of The Advocate
magazine. After months of preparation, Customs conceded the
case literally on the courthouse steps on the way to trial. We were
awarded $148.13, the cost of the magazines that had been destroyed.
A hollow victory indeed, the decision left the system of censorship
unchallenged. Changes were not made and it was business as usual
at Canada Customs. (2006: n.p.)

Even though the bookstore owners were vindicated and reimbursed for
the cost of the seized materials, the problem remained as to how to deal
with a homophobic customs regime that viewed gay and lesbian materials
as obscene. Thus began a multi-level court battle that lasted twelve years
and cost over $250,000, which proved exhausting both emotionally and
financially for the owners of the bookstore and their supporters. In the end,
according to Deva:

> Canada Customs remains free from judicial review, parliamentary
> review, or any forum in which to show Canadians that these "grave,
> systemic problems" with their bureaucracy have been amended.
> Supposedly the onus is on Customs to reveal how and what they
> changed to solve the problems, yet they remain accountable to no
> one. (2006: n.p.)

In 1988, Little Sisters owners joined with the British Columbia Civil
Liberties Association to sue the governments of Canada and British
Columbia, arguing that Canada's obscenity laws and their enforcement by
customs officials violated the equality and freedom of expression rights of
gays and lesbians (Busby 2004: 130). When the case reached the Supreme
Court, six interveners supported the appellants Little Sisters and BCCLA:
the Canadian Aids Society (CAS),[6] Canadian Civil Liberties Association
(CCLA), Canadian Conference on the Arts,[7] Equality for Gays and Lesbians
Everywhere (EGALE),[8] Women's Legal and Education Action Fund (LEAF) and
PEN Canada.[9] Two interveners supported the government: Equality Now[10]
and the Ontario government (Busby 2004).

At the Supreme Court, the issue involved the constitutionality of
the customs regime and the actions of its officials in suppressing a host
of sexually expressive material from crossing into Canada from the
United States. The material that had been seized over the years not only
included queer erotica but also ranged from sex education materials for the
community to anthologies and essay collections (LEAF Factum, *Little Sisters*,
1999: para. 6). Little Sisters was not a sex shop but rather something of a
"community centre" for "Vancouver's gay and lesbian population" (Busby
2004: 2).

The case involved an administrative document used by customs officers called the *Customs Tariff*. That document imported the definition of obscenity as provided by s. 163 of the *Criminal Code*. Little Sisters applied for declarations that Schedule VII and section 114 of the *Customs Tariff* and sections 58 and 71 of the *Customs Act* were of no force, and that the legislative provisions were construed and applied in a manner contrary to the *Canadian Charter of Rights and Freedoms*. According to Busby (2004: 134), lead counsel for LEAF:

> By the time Little Sisters reached the Supreme Court of Canada, the case presented three different issues on whether the bookstore and its owners' *Charter* rights had been violated. Had Canada Customs treated the queer bookstore in a discriminatory manner? Were the procedures used by Customs to make obscenity determinations fair? Were Canada's post-*Butler* obscenity laws unconstitutional?

Because of the complexity of these questions, *Little Sisters* was *the* case at the forefront of the anti-censorship movement in Canada (Bakan 1997: 71). It hinged on the questions of freedom of expression, the definition of obscenity and how to properly test for it, the definition of a "community" for the purposes of a community standards of tolerance test, the right to equal treatment before the law (or the right to be free from discrimination on the basis of sexual orientation or preference) and the question of the relationship between Canada Customs and the obscenity law.

In *Butler*'s aftermath, LEAF modified its position on sexually explicit expression when created by and for queer communities. This was in response to the critiques made by anti-censorship feminists to the position taken in *Butler* as well as the post-*Butler* prosecutions and border seizures. According to Busby (2004: 134), it was during the *Little Sisters* litigation that "tensions percolated... about whether and how *Butler* was affecting access to gay and lesbian materials and what contributions feminist organizations, like LEAF, would make to the case." According to Benedet (2001: 189), the underlying goal of the litigation strategy in *Little Sisters* adopted by both the bookstore owners and LEAF was "to attack the *Butler* decision by claiming that feminist arguments about pornography were wrong, and [that these arguments] inevitably provoke restrictions on the "expression" of "minority sexual practices." Of course Benedet's characterization of "feminist arguments" is not without difficulty, because it presents feminism as a monolithic voice. Indeed, the feminist argument to which Benedet (2001) refers is the argument advanced by what we have described in this book as the anti-pornography (sometimes referred to as radical) feminists, most closely associated with Catherine MacKinnon's views in favour of criminal censorship. Moreover, it is apparently also a variant of feminism to which Benedet subscribes as she acted as lead counsel to Equality Now. Equality Now intervened in support of the governments of Canada and British Columbia and advanced this radical feminist position in defence of the retention of the obscenity law and its definition established in *Butler*.

LEAF's subsequent modification of the position it had taken in *Butler*, a case which only addressed heterosexual pornography, allied them much more closely with those in the anti-censorship feminist movement, who had been very critical of LEAF's stance in the *Butler* case (Cossman et al. 1997). It was becoming more evident that the anti-censorship feminists' predictions about differential treatment of gay and lesbian sexually explicit materials had been correct. Justice Paris' decision in *R. v. Scythes*, discussed above in relation to the *Bad Attitude* prosecution, proved that point. The authorities (police and customs officers) targeted *only* gay and lesbian materials that were considered to couple sex and violence or sex with degradation and dehumanization. According to Hutchinson:

> It [was] not the peddlers of violent pornography against women that ha[d] been targeted by the authorities. The first subsequent two criminal prosecutions for obscenity were brought against a gay and lesbian bookstore. The allegedly obscene publications did not depict violence or exploitative sex, but consensual sex between people of the same gender. Of course, neither Butler nor [Catherine] MacKinnon brought about these custom seizures: they have been going on for years. But Butler did tend to validate such practices. These prosecutions are a convincing illustration of how power combines with "offensiveness" to discipline relatively vulnerable and powerless "deviant" groups by enforcing the conventional norms of acceptable behaviour. It is a chilling scenario that MacKinnon and others ignore at their peril. Indeed, the fact that some of Andrea Dworkin's books have been temporarily detained supports... this claim. (Hutchinson 1995: para. 59)

It would appear that *Butler*, which had at first glance been portrayed a victory for women's legal equality, was "quickly neutralized by bureaucratic inertia, political intransigence, judicial complacency and rank prejudice" (Hutchinson 1995: para. 59). Others would argue that it was business as usual for obscenity prosecutions (Cossman 1997; Johnson 1999).

The legal strategic debate that ensued amongst feminist scholars has been described as the Canadian follow-up to the "sex wars" — a division between "those who framed sexuality primarily as a site of danger and oppression for women and those who saw sexuality more ambivalently, as also a site of pleasure and liberation" (Cossman 2004: 851). According to Busby (2004: 134):

The interveners on Little Sisters' side all agreed, for similar reasons, with the bookstore that it had been treated with discrimination and that the procedural regime was unfair. However, while the appellants and its supporting interveners all were troubled by the post-*Butler* state of Canadian obscenity law, they differed on the problems identified and the desired outcomes.

However, there was also a divide between the arguments of the opposing feminist interveners — LEAF and Equality Now. These arguments are discussed in the next section.

Intervener Arguments in *Little Sisters*

LEAF adopted what some have called a "post-modern" (what we have called an anti-censorship) feminist position in making its intervener arguments before the Supreme Court of Canada (Cossman et al. 1997). LEAF framed its argument within the social context of cultural expression and the development of lesbian and feminist identities, sexualities, and communities, as part of its overall legal mandate to promote women's equality through law. As a public interest group, LEAF supported the retention of a harms-based approach to criminal obscenity law for both queer and heterosexual sexually explicit materials but recognized the discriminatory impact of homophobic censorship practices by Canada Customs. Similarly, EGALE argued that Customs' censorship impacted the queer community differently when those practices perpetuated the oppressive invisibility of queer communities (quoted in Busby 2004: 142). In contrast, Equality Now sought to support the use of state censorship as part of an overall strategy to promote women's equality.

Cultural Identity and Lesbophobic/
Homophobic/Heterosexist Discrimination

LEAF argued that the customs regime discriminates against lesbians by

> silencing already marginalized voices, aggravating disparities in the ability of lesbians and other women to access means of communication, and ignoring how material by, for and about lesbians connect individuals and communities and free women to shape their own lives independent of dominant norms. (LEAF Factum, *Little Sisters*, 1999: para. 13)

LEAF argued that materials about lesbians facilitated the emergence and development of lesbian identities and that therefore restrictions on access to lesbian materials made the affirmation of lesbian identity very difficult (para. 14). LEAF argued that the dominant culture sidelined queer culture and identified the heightened social problems faced by lesbians (para. 15). The availability of lesbian materials about lesbian sexuality therefore helped affirm lesbian self-exploration and played a role in creating cultural communities (para. 16). In this context, customs censorship threatened the existence of "lesbian cultural works" (para. 20). The dissemination of such materials could enhance the visibility of lesbians in the wider community and lead to increased tolerance (para. 22). According to Busby (2004: 139):

> Almost a third of LEAF's Little Sisters factum describes why materials by, for, and about lesbian women, including sexual materials, are important for the development of identities, sexualities, and communities. When magazines like *Deneuve* and *The Advocate* and works by Jane Rule, the Kiss and Tell Collective, bell hooks, Sarah Schulman, Dorothy Allison, Susie Bright and Pat Califia, to name just a few, are seized repeatedly by Canada Customs, lesbian and feminist culture are clearly under attack.

In this regard, it was LEAF's position that equality rights of heterosexual women are actually enhanced by the dissemination of lesbian materials because such materials may challenge "sexism, compulsory heterosexuality and the dominant, heterosexist sexual representations which often portray 'normal' heterosexuality as men dominating women and women enjoying pain and degradation" (para. 24).

LEAF argued that certain principles of substantive equality ought to be incorporated into obscenity law since "obscenity law is constitutionally valid only if it is anchored in a fully developed equality analysis which acknowledges both the liberatory and oppressive possibilities of sexual materials for and about adults" (para. 25). LEAF contended that a more politically sensitive application of *Butler* was now required to account for the expressive value of queer pornography. In particular, LEAF and the other queer sensitive interveners argued that there needed to be a recognition of the "differential impact that obscenity law has on queer and BDSM (bondage, domination/ submission, and sadomasochism) materials when developing and applying obscenity jurisprudence to take into account the fact that the materials are not understood by more readers or viewers" (Busby 2004: 144). In that regard, LEAF challenged the suitability of the customs regime for making obscenity determinations, particularly since it had been demonstrated over and over again that customs officers were unable to prohibit materials in a constitutionally sensitive manner (cited in Busby 2004: 144).

Section 1 of the *Charter* requires the government to establish "that the limits it imposes are in response to a pressing and substantial objective and that the means used to achieve this objective are rationally connected to the objective and minimally impair the rights of those affected" (Busby 2004: 145). CAS and EGALE argued that the customs regime ought to be struck down because the government had failed to establish that it met this test. In other words, the government did not adequately justify the customs' infringement upon Little Sisters. However, unlike the litigants, the queer sensitive interveners did not locate the problem in respect of the obscenity law itself, but rather in its application by customs. Thus, according to Busby (2004: 145), the lack of rational objective *coupled* with "a draconian legislative regime, which suppresses a disproportionately large amount of homo-erotic publications, including an alarming quantity of materials that do not satisfy the statutory definition of 'obscene'" (EGALE Factum *Little Sisters* 1999: 38) provided the justification to strike down the whole regime. The litigants argued for a categorical exemption for gay and lesbian pornography (including violent and degrading and dehumanizing pornography) due to a lack of power imbalance between sexual actors, whereas the queer sensitive interveners focused on the misadministration of the law by the customs officers. In its decision, the Supreme Court would reject the litigants' argument for a categorical exemption of queer pornography, instead reiterating the *Butler* standard.

LEAF's Harm-Based Critique of the Community Standards Test

LEAF argued that the Court ought to reject the community standards test because it failed to provide the appropriate avenue for assessing whether the materials in question cause a substantial risk of harm or whether they have merit (para. 40). Merit is determined by the "internal necessities test," which establishes whether targeted materials have artistic, literary, scientific or educational merit. In addition to maintaining that customs officers have little or no ability to determine the artistic, literary, scientific or education merit of the materials they routinely seize from Little Sisters, LEAF argued that community standards are majoritarian standards and therefore likely to facilitate the importation of anti-lesbian attitudes into the heart of obscenity law (para. 42). In this regard, LEAF picked up on Cossman's (1997: 132–34) critique of the community standards test levelled earlier in response to the *Butler* decision. According to Cossman (1997: 134):

> The test for community standards is supposed to be formally neutral to sexual orientation. But what this standard of formal neutrality obscures is the extent to which the standard is one deeply informed by heterosexual assumptions. The community standard is a heterosexual standard, and it is this heterosexual standard that becomes the norm by which all representations of sexuality are to be judged.

Because there exist homophobic attitudes towards gays and lesbians these attitudes may be imported through the majoritarian community standards test, resulting in gay and lesbian materials being deemed to be "obscene." Therefore, LEAF emphasized the importance of a harms-based obscenity law rooted in evidence of harm. This emphasis would later get picked up by the Supreme Court in *R. v. Labaye* [2005]. A harm-based approach must, according to LEAF, consider

> the sex, race, age, disability, and sexual orientation of the participants, characters, and the creators; the purposes of the materials; the intended audience; real or apparent violence; consent and dialogue; the nature of the publication, including the relationship of the impugned materials to the entirety of the publication; the framework and manner of production, distribution and consumption, and the benefits to viewers/readers from the production and dissemination of the materials. (para. 30)

For LEAF, the justification for state intervention or censorship must be based on *evidence* of harm and lack of *merit* (para. 29).[11]

The Supreme Court Decision and Analysis in Little Sisters

Unlike the interveners, the owners of Little Sisters sought a categorical exemption for queer pornography from the obscenity law. The main argument advanced by the litigants in support of the gay and lesbian materials that failed the *Butler* test (for coupling same-sex with violence and for coupling same-sex with degradation and dehumanization) was that gay and lesbian sex is "different" from heterosexual sex mainly because structural inequality between the sexes was not an issue in these depictions. Put another way, absent structural inequalities produced by gender inequality, sexual practices that depicted one person being violent towards another, or degrading and dehumanizing another, contributed to no inequalities in queer communities and should therefore be tolerated by Canadian society under the community standards of tolerance test as set out in *Butler.*

Little Sisters bookstore owners and their supporting interveners argued that the community standards of tolerance test either needed to be applied so as to account for the unique situation of queer communities or was not the appropriate test to apply to queer communities. In part, the argument was an attempt to address the issue of homophobia and to re-frame the community standards test to account for minority sexual practices that *might* be considered "obscene" by homophobic persons. The bookstore owners argued that those violent and degrading and dehumanizing sexually explicit queer materials (BDSM materials) resulted in actualization through sexual affirmation of the targeted community and could benefit the targeted community. The current practice of BDSM can be traced to the sexual liberation movements of the 1960s, but emerged in gay and lesbian communities in the 1980s in the context of the AIDS epidemic, which required safer sex practices (BCCLA 2006: 3). Despite the fact that "BDSM and fetish imagery is now widespread in Western mainstream culture, from Robert Mapplesthorpe's photographs, to Madonna's music videos" and that the "psychological and psychiatric mainstream no longer views sadomasochistic behaviour as pathological," the "courts have largely been unwilling to view BDSM as an acceptable practice — in Canada, engaging in BDSM activities is subject to criminal sanction." (BCCLA 2006: 4–5). This is especially the case with respect to sexually explicit materials aimed at a queer consumer. None of these materials aimed at a heterosexual audience have been targeted for prosecution.

The *Little Sisters* case was viewed as at least a partial victory because the Court found the actions of customs officials to be discriminatory (LEAF Media Release 2000). In *Little Sisters*, the Supreme Court ruled that the bookstore owners suffered differential treatment when compared to importers of heterosexually explicit material who also carried at least some of the same titles as Little Sisters bookstore. Therefore, the Court ruled the discretion exercised by customs officers violated the equality guaranteed under s.15 of the *Charter*. However, in keeping with the history of obscenity jurisprudence described above, the Court underscored the importance of the established community standards test to ensure the proper functioning of society:

> The interpretation given to s. 163(8) of the *Criminal Code* in *Butler* does not discriminate against the gay and lesbian community. The national community standard of tolerance relates to harm, not taste, and is restricted to conduct which society formally recognizes as incompatible with its proper functioning. While it is true that under s. 163(8) the "community standard" is identified by a jury or a judge sitting alone, a concern for minority expression is one of the principal factors that led to adoption [sic] of the national community test in Butler in the first place. The Canadian community specifically recognized in the Charter that equality (and with it, the protection of sexual minorities) is one of the fundamental values of Canadian society. The standard of tolerance of this same Canadian community for obscenity cannot reasonably be interpreted as seeking to suppress sexual expression in the gay and lesbian community in a discriminatory way. Butler validates a broad range of sexually explicit expression as non-harmful. (*Little Sisters Book and Art Emporium v. Canada (Minister of Justice)* 2000: at headnote)

In this regard, the Court rejected the argument that community standards are majoritarian standards and that they import homophobia into the heart of obscenity law:

This line of criticism underestimates *Butler*. While it is of course true that under s. 163 of the *Criminal Code* the "community standard" is identified by a jury or a judge sitting alone, and to that extent involves an attribution rather than an opinion poll, the test was adopted to underscore the unacceptability of the trier of fact indulging personal biases, as was held to have happened in *Towne Cinema, supra*. A concern for minority expression is one of the principal factors that led to adoption of the national community test in *Butler* in the first place. (para. 56)

In other words, obscenity is obscenity regardless of whether it takes the form of heterosexual pornography or gay and lesbian pornography. The Court simply re-affirmed the longstanding juridical position that the test for obscenity is aimed at criminalizing expression that is incompatible with the proper functioning of Canadian society and that it must be applied equally to all groups in society.

In other words, a person's constitutionally protected space does not shrink by virtue of his or her geographical location or participation in a certain context or community, or indeed by the taste of a particular judge or jury. It is not necessarily in the interest of the minority to disaggregate community standards. The appellants have in mind a special standard related to their lesbian and gay target audience. The fact is, however, that they operate a bookstore in a very public place open to anyone who happens by, including potentially outraged individuals of the local community who might wish to have the bookstore closed down altogether. If "special standards" are to apply, whose "special standard" is it to be? There is some safety in numbers, and a national constituency that is made up of many different minorities is a guarantee of tolerance for minority expression. (para. 57)

Therefore, the government was found to be in the wrong because it applied the harms-based test in a *discriminatory* way towards gay and lesbian sexually explicit materials not because the test itself discriminated against gays and lesbians as a sexual minority group (para. 58). In other words, just as heterosexuals deserve protection from "obscenity" to preserve society, gays and lesbians also deserved protection from "obscenity." The Court even rejected the argument that the community standards test for "degrading and dehumanizing" materials could easily find gay and lesbian materials "obscene" because homophobics find same-sex practices morally repugnant:

The appellants argue that the "degrading or dehumanizing" language in *Butler* is highly subjective and encouraged Customs, for example, to prohibit depictions of anal intercourse long after the Department of Justice advised Customs to the contrary. This argument seems to ignore that the phrase "degrading or dehumanizing" in *Butler* is qualified immediately by the words "if the risk of harm is substantial" (p. 485 (emphasis added)). This makes it clear that not all sexually explicit erotica depicting adults engaged in conduct which is considered to be degrading or dehumanizing is obscene. The material must also create a substantial risk of harm which exceeds the community's tolerance. The potential of harm and a same-sex depiction are not necessarily mutually exclusive. Portrayal of a dominatrix engaged in the non-violent degradation of an ostensibly willing sex slave is no less dehumanizing if the victim happens to be of the same sex, and no less (and no more) harmful in its reassurance to the viewer that the victim finds such conduct both normal and pleasurable. Parliament's concern was with behavioural changes in the *voyeur* that are potentially harmful in ways or to an extent that the community is not prepared to tolerate. There is no reason to restrict that concern to the heterosexual community. (para. 60)

In this respect, the Court rejects any notion that the test *itself* (as opposed to its discriminatory application by customs officers) is morality in disguise because of the exclusive focus on *harm*. In other words, the harms-based test established in *Butler* is not a morality test, as the bookstore owners had asserted:

This line of argument simply rejects the idea that *Butler* means what it says, i.e., that the community standard of tolerance is based on the reasonable apprehension of harm, not on morality. The arguments assume that any appeal to a national community standard cannot be targeted on harm and will inevitably be overwhelmed by majoritarian taste. This approach presupposes that the arbiter (the broader community) is incapable of being focussed on the task that it is required to address (harm). We have no evidence that the courts are not able to apply the *Butler* test, and the reported decisions seem to confirm that the identification of harm is a well understood requirement: *R. v. Hawkins* (1993), 15 O.R. (3d) 549 (C.A.), at p. 566; *R. v. Jacob* (1996), 112 C.C.C. (3d) 1 (Ont. C.A.), a case of alleged indecent exposure; and *R. v. Erotica Video Exchange Ltd.* (1994), 163 A.R. 181 (Prov. Ct.). (para. 62)[12]

Despite the functionalist assumptions inherent to the community standards of tolerance test, it nevertheless provided the opportunity for multiple voices to be heard at the Supreme Court. A wide array of disparate viewpoints of special interest intervener groups made up a significant part of the *Little Sisters* case. Nowlin (2003) argues that the submissions to Canada's highest Court was a discursive moment in the history of evidence — a moment where fact finding had never been more informed by expert witnesses and social scientific materials. The *Little Sisters* case provided the opportunity for queer and feminist articulations of a variety of legal arguments and academic debates about censorship in Canada.[13] This debate would eventually be foreclosed by the Court's 2005 decision to abandon the community standards test for obscenity and indecency in *R. v. Labaye*. We discuss that decision in the next chapter.

Notes

1. The BC Civil Liberties Association (BCCLA) was established in 1962 and is the oldest and most active civil liberties group in Canada. It is funded by the Law Foundation of B.C. and by citizens. See <bccla.org/05about.htm>.
2. See Johnson (1995) for a general discussion of harm.
3. *R. v. Scythes*, OCJ, 16 February 1993.
4. See also editorial, "Reading between the Borderlines," *Globe and Mail*, June 30, 1992.
5. See also LEAF News Release, "Historic Gathering Condemns Targeting of Lesbian and Gay Materials and Sex Trade Workers," Toronto, June 21, 1993.
6. On its website, the Society notes that it advocates "on behalf of people and communities affected by HIV/AIDS, facilitate the development of programs, services and resources for our member groups, and provide a national framework for community-based participation in Canada's response to AIDS." See <http://www.cdnaids.ca/web/casmisc.nsf/cl/cas-gen-0049!opendocument&language=english>.
7. According to their website, the Canadian Conference of the Arts (CCA) "is the national forum for the arts and cultural community in Canada. It provides research, analysis and consultations on public policies affecting the arts and the Canadian cultural institutions and industries. The CCA fosters informed public debate on policy issues and seeks to advance the cultural rights of Canadians." See <http://www.ccarts.ca/en/>.
8. According to its website: "EGALE Canada was founded in 1986 to advance equality for Canadian lesbian, gay, bisexual and transgendered people and their families, across Canada. Our work includes: carrying out political action to lobby for more equitable laws for LGBT people; intervening in legal cases that have an impact on human rights and equality; increasing public education and awareness by providing information to individuals, groups and media." See <http://www.egale.ca/index.asp?lang=E and menu=2 and item=762>.
9. According to its webpage "PEN Canada works on behalf of writers, at home and abroad, who have been forced into silence for writing the truth as they see it. PEN Canada is for debate and against silence. We lobby governments in Canada and internationally; organize petitions; send letters, faxes and postcards for the release

of persecuted writers; and conduct public awareness campaigns about freedom of expression. We work for the release of imprisoned writers internationally, against censorship nationally and for networking and professional opportunities for writers living in exile in Canada." See <http://www.pencanada.ca/about/index.php.>.

10. On its website Equality Now states that it "was founded in 1992 to work for the protection and promotion of the human rights of women around the world. Working with national human rights organizations and individual activists, Equality Now documents violence and discrimination against women and mobilizes international action to support their efforts to stop these human rights abuses." See <http://www.equalitynow.org/english/about/about_en.html>.

11. The Supreme Court in *R. v. Labaye* [2005] would later incorporate a anti-pornography feminist position on the issue of evidence of harm.

12. The Court did find the reverse onus scheme, which puts the onus of proof on the bookstore owners to establish that seized materials *are not* obscene, rather than on the government to prove that they *are* obscene, to be constitutionally unjustifiable.

13. See also Cossman (2003), Kendall (2004a, 2004b), Benedet (2001), Pickel (2001), Sumner (2004), the policy musings of Ryder (2003), Mathen (2001), Zanghellini (2004). These authors provide arguments around the establishment of a harms-based test to promote women's equality in the Canadian obscenity context.

Chapter Three

Labaye: Hicklin's
Modern Swinging Cousin

After the landmark Canadian case of *R. v. Butler* [1992], the Canadian approach to obscenity and indecency law was at the centre of a North American Anglo-feminist debate surrounding "obscenity." Some Anglo American feminists' reaction to the arguments presented in the case, and the decision itself, were optimistic since the case seemed to consider the equality interests of women as central to the interrogation of the harms caused by sexually explicit expression (MacKinnon 1993; Scales 1994; Strossen 1995). Yet others, within the Anglo Canadian feminist legal community, greeted the decision with more scepticism, seeing the use of harm in this context as more equivocal in regards to the socio-political context of women (Cossman, Bell, Gotell and Ross 1997; Valverde 1999). Thirteen years later, in 2005, the Supreme Court of Canada revisited the obscenity and indecency issue; this time it ruled on the question of whether the Montréal sex club, Le loft de l'Orage (l'Orage) (translated into English, as the Storm Club), violated the Canadian bawdy house provision of section 210(1) of the *Criminal Code* for "indecency."

Owned and operated by Jean-Paul Labaye, l'Orage charged admission fees for swingers sex parties and other themed sex parties, which included "Voyeur–Exhibitionist" sex play on Fridays and Fetish Play Parties on Saturdays (including BDSM). Club L'Orage, recently re-opened, advertises itself as world renowned for legalizing swingers sex clubs in Canada as a result of the Supreme Court decision in *R. v. Labaye* [2005], which overturned Labaye's conviction. In that decision, the Court reconfigured the existing community standards of tolerance test for obscenity (expressive and depicted sexuality such as pornography) and indecency (sexually explicit conduct as opposed to expression) in Canada (Jochelson 2009a, 2009b).

A differently configured Supreme Court, led by Conservative government appointee the Right Honourable Chief Justice Beverly McLachlin, reinterpreted and inscribed a harms-based approach to regulating indecency and obscenity. The Court a) sought factual evidence of harm (though we argue this demand is equivocal); b) created conditions for criminalizing potential harm through a discourse of *risk* of harm; and c) abandoned the community standards of tolerance test for undue exploitation of *Butler*, replacing it with a more abstract test for risk of harm and harm. In this case, the harm is deployed to justify criminal sanction rather than to oppose restrictions on individual freedom or justify censorship to promote women's equality interests. This "new" test links criminal regulation to liberal moral and political principles, a move that has the potential to limit freedom by appealing to uninterrogated societal norms. Despite the Court's demand for positive knowledge of harm and risk of harm, *Labaye* operationalizes an autocratic test much like its predecessors in that it is devoted mainly to protecting a normative vision of society. The jurisprudence presumes that the social terrain into which government can intercede to manage and protect is a consensual moral order characterized by autonomy, liberty and equality. This constructed society is *threatened* by obscenity and indecency. Inequalities and marginalization are not seen as structural social phenomena but rather as risks to prevent. This brings a particular sexual subject into existence — women and other sexual minorities who are objects engaging in sexual activities for commercial consumption; the inherent logic assumes that *proper society* must be protected from the risks of exposure to these populations. With respect to indecency, it is indeed women as sex trade workers who will be the criminalized "other" and who pose a risk of harming the proper functioning of society; the threat is constructed as more acute when the conduct is of a sexually explicit nature and is determined to have taken place in "public," thereby interfering with "our" autonomy and liberty (*R. v. Labaye* 2005: para. 62).

One of our broad goals in the work so far has been to show that each iteration of the "obscenity and indecency harm technology" asserts dominion over "corrupt" fixed norms to buttress the proper functioning of a society. This general trend continues in *Labaye* but is reconstituted in a more direct fashion. By directing our attention toward society's proper functioning, the reasoning in *Labaye* subverts open debate about the multiple meanings of indecency and obscenity and thus obscures, for example, the consideration of socio-political contexts particular to populations such as sex trade workers and queer communities (ignoring, for example, that the activities or speech might be viewed as liberatory in some circumstances). What is more, *risk of harm* is deployed as something tangible in *Labaye*, forming part of *actus reus* for criminal liability (the criminal act which the Crown must prove in criminal trials) for both indecency and obscenity.

The law of evidence in Canada as established in *R. v. Mohan* [1993] allows for judicial risk and harm determinations without reliance upon expert opinion evidence, obviating the need to prove risk of harm and harm beyond a reasonable doubt using evidentiary standards. *Mohan* was a Supreme Court case which provided that the opinion of the experts must be necessary in the sense that "it provides information which is likely to be outside the experience or knowledge of a judge or jury" (*R. v. Mohan* 1993: para. 22). The Court in *Mohan* was concerned that an over-reliance on the use of expert witnesses could "usurp the functions of the trier of fact," so that a judge or jury's decision could be subject to political persuasion (para. 24). Thus, we are left with a situation in which the judge cannot be persuaded from her normative imperative even when an entire population, for instance, an entire community, dissents. The *Labaye* harm-based test shifts the balance of power towards the judiciary and away from communities of experts in the human sciences, sex trade workers and sexual minorities. As we demonstrate through our discussion of *R. v. Sheikh* [2008] below (an indecency case following *R. v. Labaye*), social scientific expertise (knowledge of harm) is not required for a court that sees both moral and political danger when sexual activities take place in public spaces.

We view the juridical test established in *R. v. Labaye* as the evolution of a normalizing political strategy wherein private/public sexual relations are governed through those norms that make up the "properly functioning society." Viewed from this vantage point, each iteration of the harm-based test is what Bauman refers to as the imposition of a norm that reflects a model of order that is projected onto human conduct: "The norm tells people what it means to behave in an orderly fashion in a well-ordered society — it translates, so to speak, the concept of order into the language of human choices" (2000: 24). By abandoning the community standards of tolerance approach, the test shifts away from multi-vocality towards abstraction.

In the first part of this chapter, we continue outlining phases of the Court's operationalization of harm technology for regulating the obscene and the indecent. We have already discussed the (1) the *Hicklin* era (1868–1962); (2) the community standards era (1962–1992); and (3) the *Butler/Little Sisters* era (1992–2005). In this chapter we consider the operationalization of the *Butler* era in the context of indecency and the reformation of that approach in the "factual harm" era (2005–present). We then undertake an analysis of *Labaye*, in particular, of how the Court extended the common law conception of the harm caused by obscenity and indecency to include risk of harm.

In the latter half of this chapter, we argue that the *Labaye* test follows a particular logic that has been described as an "illiberal" use of harm-based tests (Smith 2006: 3) and that others locate in the context of the "risk" society (Castel 1991; Hudson 2003; O'Malley 1996, 2004; Stenson and Sullivan 2001). We have already suggested that the Court's rationality presumes consensual moral order. Now *risk* of harm (which encapsulates *potential* harms, which may or may not be quantifiable or tangible) expands the conceptual and practical terrain into which the state can use the harm technology. This jurisprudential strategy of risk management adds another layer to debates about the direct (often tangible, such as "physical") and indirect (often intangible, such as "dehumanization-based") harms of obscenity and indecency, which have been well articulated in the literature (see Koppelman 2005). Potential harm is neither putatively tangible nor intangible, since threat to society's proper functioning is viewed as worthy of prevention. The expansion of the harm test to imagine threats of harm as a justifiable exercise of state sanction has been achieved without much criticism. The addition of the category of risk as a basis for criminal regulation enables the deployment of imagined effects of obscenity and indecency (*potential* attitudinal harm) as the basis for penal sanction. This development might seem attractive from a political activist perspective, yet it nevertheless empowers the judiciary to promote the constitutional values of liberty, autonomy and perhaps equality through punishment on the basis of little or no empirical evidence of harm caused by obscenity and indecency. This also allows a court the luxury of avoiding any criticism of the relationship between punishment and the protection of constitutional values — what matters is that society function properly and such functioning assumes constitutional fidelity. Finally, we argue that the use of risk when paired with the type of "objectivity" inscribed by the *Labaye* Court allows for decontextualized articulations of harm. When harm is constructed on the basis of a notion of an objective legal test (the new harm test) rather than contextualized subjectivities (the community standards test), it may be easier to claim that risk of harm is imminent, and criminal conviction may be more likely, even in cases where the sexual conduct or materials under review (indecency or obscenity) might have multiple meanings in diverse sexual populations. For example, the voices of queer communities in the context of erotica aimed at those communities are secondary under the *Labaye* formulation to the Court's construction of society's proper functioning.

If, as is the case in *Labaye*, that functioning is constructed by reference to a universalized empirical standard, dissenting voices are obfuscated and the notion of "proper functioning" is constructed mono-vocally, using only a court's voice and its appreciation of, at the least, risk of harm. After *Labaye*, when the loss of context combines with risk, we lament a return to the determination of obscenity and indecency with the "I know it when I see it" approach to legal analysis; the key discursive turn is that "it" is now harm or risk of harm.

Indecency: The Private/Public Debate

The operationalization of the community standards of tolerance test for establishing harm occur in the context of the indecency provisions of the *Code* — i.e., where bawdy houses are being run for the purposes of indecency or where indecent performances are being held. In *R. v. Tremblay* [1993], the Court considered whether the accused were running a common bawdy house. In this case, nude dancers performed in individual cubicles for clients and would assume a number of sexually suggestive positions. Masturbating by the customer was tolerated by the proprietors as was clothing removal, though a "no touching the dancers" policy persisted. The Court confirmed that the meaning of indecency was given content by the *Butler* test of harm (*Tremblay* 1993: para. 55). The Court cited *Butler* approvingly:

> The courts must determine as best they can what the community would tolerate others being exposed to on the basis of the degree of harm that may flow from such exposure. Harm in this context means that it predisposes persons to act in an anti-social manner as, for example, the physical or mental mistreatment of women by men, or, what is perhaps debatable, the reverse. Anti-social conduct for this purpose is conduct which society formally recognizes as incompatible with its proper functioning.... Similarly evidence as to the community standards is desirable but not essential. (para. 58, citing *Butler* 1992: 485)

In considering whether acts of public masturbation and sexual dancing violated the community standards of tolerance test, the Court considered a range of social scientific evidence including testimony of an expert on human sexual behaviour and attitudes and the Fraser Committee Report on Pornography and Prostitution. With this research in mind, the Court surmised that the acts of public masturbation and sexual dancing would fall within the range of community standards of tolerance. However, the Court then considered the surrounding circumstances in respect of the dancing that were unique to the case (paras. 60–69, 81–82). The Court considered the lack of physical contact and low risk of transmission of sexual disease (*R. v. Tremblay* 1993: paras. 82–84), and the private nature of the activity (paras. 85–87). The Court noted that the peep-holes on the doors of private rooms were being used for safety purposes rather than public voyeurism, thus making the dancing less harmful and, therefore, presumptively tolerable. The Court found that no harm or risk of harm was caused by the activities (para. 88). Here the notion that criminal law can regulate potential harm emerges. Lastly, the Court considered that the acts were consensual and that there were no complaints from clients or nearby residents. The dancing in this case was very similar to a "run of the mill" strip club (paras. 89–91). Thus, the Court concluded that the performances of the dancers were accepted by the public and the police, and since the actions were non-violent that they should be tolerated by the community.

In *R. v. Mara* [1997], the Court considered whether sexual performances, for a fee, were indecent. The acts in question were essentially lap dancing intermingled with conduct ranging from breast fondling to cunnilingus. The Court once again confirmed that indecency was constituted by undertaking the *Butler* test, while having regard to the circumstances in which a potentially indecent act took place, in order to determine whether the community would tolerate the act (*R. v. Mara* 1997: para. 33). The relevant social harm considered by the Court was the attitudinal harm suffered by those watching the performances as perceived by the community as a whole (para. 34). The Court distinguished this case from cases such as *Tremblay* on the basis that *Tremblay* was considering whether acts performed in a private room were indecent whereas *Mara* was concerned with whether a public performance was indecent. The presence of multiple spectators in a performance changed the emphasis of the harm analysis (para. 39–40). The public nature of the act coupled with physical contact with the dancers made this context factually different from previous indecency cases.

The Court noted that social harm was not susceptible of proof in the traditional way, but rather rested upon whether the activities involved the degradation and objectification of women, or perhaps children or men; the law may infer harm simply from that degradation and objectification. Thus, the question of harm was a legal question that the Court could both construct and answer (para. 44). The Court argued that indecency depended on community standards, which depended largely on its own analysis of social harm (para. 45). The Court characterized the minimization of the risk of sexually transmitted diseases as having little weight but nonetheless found the activities to violate the community standards of tolerance test, rendering the performances indecent (para. 57). In other words, the women's working conditions were irrelevant to indecency and the focus was instead placed upon the negative effects in terms of the potential anti-social behaviour of men, or more generally, societal harm (Johnson 1999: 311). However, on separate grounds, the Court found that the appellant did not possess the necessary mental element to be found guilty of a criminally indecent performance.

The "Factual Harm" Era (2005–present)

Academics grew increasingly sceptical of the utility of the community standards of tolerance test, as did potential litigants and offenders (Cossman et al. 1997; Cossman 2004; Valverde, 1999; Sumner 2004; Ryder 2003). Others steadfastly maintained that the *Butler* test was a victory for all Canadian equality-seeking communities (Benedet 2001; Kendall 2004a, 2004b). Ultimately, in *R. v. Labaye*, the Supreme Court retired the community standards of tolerance test and in its place suggested a juridical harm-based test for assessing criminal liability for obscenity and indecency. The case seemed to suggest an increased evidentiary foundation for establishing criminal liability in the context of indecency and obscenity to achieve an "objective" test.

In *R. v. Labaye*, the accused was charged with keeping a common bawdy-house for the practice of acts of indecency under s. 210(1) of the *Criminal Code*, which provides that "Every one who keeps a common bawdy-house is guilty of an indictable offence and liable to imprisonment for a term not exceeding two years." The accused operated a club in Montreal which permitted couples and single people to meet each other for group sex. The majority decided that the community standards of tolerance test would be replaced with a harm-based standard. Indeed, the majority suggested that this was a shift that had already been completed by the time *Little Sisters* was decided.

The majority noted that the community standards of tolerance test was an attempt to cleanse the assessment of obscenity from the "idiosyncrasies and the subjective moral views of the judge or jurors" and what they determined was capable of corrupting influence (*R. v. Labaye* 2005: para. 16). Although the community standards test was seen as objective at the time, requiring the trier of fact to determine what the community would tolerate, the *Labaye* Court's majority argued that the concept of a national community standard of tolerance proved difficult to apply in an objective fashion (para. 18).

The majority cited pointed critiques of the community standards of tolerance test. First, the Court determined that evidence of what a community would tolerate was spurious at best. Second, the Court doubted that a single community could be constructed in as multi-cultural and plural a society as Canada — such a standard was unworkable. Last, the Court wondered how one could assume a community would tolerate something if in reality the community never could have or would have considered the issue; one cannot objectively determine what the community would tolerate "in the absence of evidence that the community knew of and considered the conduct at issue." The result was a test whose conduct was dictated by personal viewpoints; those of experts, judges and jurors. The objectivity of the test had been unduly and accidentally compromised (para. 18).

Nonetheless, the majority argued that in *Butler* and *Little Sisters*, the substance of the test was harm-based. Those Courts decided that one must determine as best as one can what the community would tolerate others being exposed to "on the basis of the degree of harm that may flow from such exposure." What was harm in this context? Harm was when materials predisposed persons to act anti-socially. Anti-social behaviour was conduct that society formally recognized (through the *Constitution* or other fundamental moral documents (para. 36) as incompatible with its proper functioning. The new test would create a binary sexual category (normal/deviant) based on a seemingly "objective" analysis of harm. The analysis must establish a substantial inference of harm or risk of harm from the material in question to the proper functioning of society. The functionalist normativity of the Court was revealed for all to read (paras. 21–22).

For a finding of criminality in indecency and obscenity, the majority proposed analyzing first the nature of the harm and second the degree of harm. Three types of harm had emerged from the case law: harm to those whose autonomy and liberty was restricted by being confronted with "inappropriate" conduct; harm to society by predisposing others to anti-social conduct; and harm to individuals participating in the conduct (para. 36). The harm to the liberty interests of the passerby was akin to the right to be free from materials that constituted a sexual nuisance; freedom to live free from deep offence in one's routine and daily activities. There may be "some kinds of sexual conduct" which "seriously impairs the liveability of the environment and significantly constrains autonomy" (para. 41). The risk of harm in these cases must be that members are unwillingly exposed to conduct or material resulting in a significant shift of usual conduct, which would require an assessment of the manner, place and audience of the expression/conduct. In this regard, the jurisprudence shifts towards managing criminogenic situations and events and abandons the kind of concern with individual pathology more clearly articulated in *Hicklin*.

The analysis of harm to society by predisposing others to anti-social conduct was the harm most often associated with the promulgation of "pornography" throughout society and with sexually explicit conduct. A condition precedent to establishing this kind of harm was that the display or conduct was public (para. 47). The Court admitted that this type of harm was Hicklinesque in that it was concerned with "depraving and corrupting susceptible people." However, the causal threshold was higher under *Butler* though "the logic [was] the same: in some cases, the criminal law may limit conduct and expression in order to prevent people who may see it from becoming predisposed to acting in an anti-social manner" (para. 45).

The analysis of harm to participants would include physical or psychological harm to individuals involved in the conduct or expression at issue. Such harms include those types of sexual activities that were not a "positive source of human expression, fulfillment and pleasure." Amongst the harms postulated were forced prostitution, sex slavery, assault and death. Such harms could occur to women and similarly to "children and men" (para. 48).

Once a type of harm has been established, the degree of harm must be assessed. One would need to determine whether the material or conduct was incompatible with the proper functioning of society (para. 52). This would require an assessment of harm on the basis of factual evidence and with a full appreciation of "the relevant factual and legal context, to ensure that it is informed not by the judge's subjective views, but by relevant, objectively tested criteria" (para. 54).

In balancing the unwanted interference with liberty, the Crown must establish a real risk that the way people live their lives will be adversely affected; the number of people affected would be crucial, and the effect on those already willingly participating or watching would not be considered criminal harm, presumably because they are already "damaged" (para. 57). For harms based on predisposing others to anti-social behaviour, a link must be established "first between the sexual conduct at issue and the formation of negative attitudes, and second between those attitudes and real risk of anti-social behaviour" (para. 58). For participatory harms, real harm must be demonstrated through the use of witnesses or expert witnesses and the evidence may be about risk of harm; vulnerability of the participants would be considered when necessary (para. 59).

In most cases, expert evidence would help to establish any of the alleged harms, but when the Crown relies on establishing a risk of harm rather than an actual harm, such evidence may be absent (para. 60). Yet, "the more extreme the nature of the harm, the lower the degree of risk that may be required to [be proven]." A terrorist attack, for instance, would mandate a less strained evidentiary threshold of harm than brief nudity on television, and in such cases criminality could be more easily established. Proving harm beyond a reasonable doubt would require that "the nature of the harm engendered by sexual conduct will require at least a probability that the risk will develop to justify convicting and imprisoning those engaged in or facilitating the conduct." (para. 61).

The majority in *Labaye* found that the autonomy and liberty of members of the public were not affected in the context of the swingers club because everyone involved was willing and consensual. Further, only those already disposed to swinging were allowed to participate and watch, a matter guaranteed by membership fees, code-locked doors and screening meetings with potential club members. There was also no evidence of anti-social acts or attitudes toward women or even men. No one was coerced or goaded into sex, no one paid for or was paid for sex, and no one was treated as a "mere sexual object for the gratification of others" (paras. 66–71; see also *Kouri* [2005]). Had any such juridical harms existed, the Court believed that, in any event, such harms were compatible with the proper functioning of society because "consensual conduct behind code locked doors can hardly be supposed to jeopardize a society as vigorous and tolerant as Canadian society."

Labaye's Functionalism

Through the *Labaye* decision, the Court developed a "workable theory of harm" (*R. v. Labaye* 2005: para. 26) "grounded in norms which our society has recognized in its Constitution or similar fundamental laws" (para. 29). This theory of harm connects the exercise of state power to the proper functioning of society that is damaged when actual harm to an individual's or society's political values are deemed to have been affronted by obscenity and/or indecency (para. 30). Criminal responsibility is determined on the basis of whether the impugned materials or acts are incompatible with the proper functioning of society (para. 32).

The *Labaye* Court's new harm-based test, which abandons a consideration of the community's ostensible tolerance, establishes on the one hand that a putative factual basis must exist for a harm to trigger state intervention. The subject of the community standards test was what the reasonable (and "ordinary") member of the community would *tolerate* of others, and not what they themselves would or would not tolerate. The courts never used to ask whether a member of the community would themselves consume the impugned material; instead they asked whether the material *ought* to be tolerated. For this reason, some feminist commentators objected to the community standards test because it allowed for the tolerance of sexually explicit materials and practices that undermined women's equality, which they viewed as morally offensive (Benedet 2001). From this perspective, the community standards test was too lax. The new *Labaye* test removes adjudication from the terrain of tolerance for others being exposed to certain materials into the terrain of identifying harm to abstract political values like equality. The obscenity and indecency question has been reduced not to a tolerant (or intolerant) community but to a question of *harm* to individuals or society in a way that actually undermines or threatens to undermine a value formally endorsed through the Constitution such as equality (para. 62). In that regard, the new rationality justifies criminalization on the grounds that it offends liberal ideology. In addition, even a *risk* of harm to the value of equality could presumably justify censorship and criminal sanction. This solves the problem for some feminist commentators and those who objected to the old community standards test, because their vision of equality may in some cases be achievable under the new functionalism, though it is not foundational under such an approach (Craig 2008).

Nevertheless, the new harm test continues to invite judges to interpose their own values because the trier of fact is not *required* to weigh social scientific evidence of harm under the Court's own rules of evidence as established in *R. v. Mohan* [1994]. We argue that this leaves us with the potential for triers of fact to impute "moral danger" (in the language of risk of harm and harm) when courts ought to be required to weigh factual evidence about moral questions. Political intervention is also justified on the basis of uninterrogated assumptions about the connections between pornography and the sex trade and harm to liberalism itself. Thus, *Labaye* returns us to the world of corrupting influences articulated in *Hicklin*, and yet obfuscates, or at least makes secondary, the equality/harm pairing yearned for and detected by some in *Butler*.

Thus, in *Labaye*, the Court achieves a kind of disambiguation of harm from the promotion of substantive equality, an approach that was possible under *Butler* and alluded to in *Little Sisters*. Now, all harms (predisposition harms, liberal affronts and participatory harms) must be linked to both harm to and risk of harm to the proper functioning of society, which will establish the *actus reus* for indecency and obscenity. However, the sort of harm the Court is acutely focused on is linked only to the proper functioning of society, which is at the nucleus of the test. This sort of harm is acknowledged to be Hicklinesque, but the Court nonetheless claims to cleanse the taint of *Hicklin*-style corruptibility by clinging to its objectivity and other evidentiary contortions. According to the reasoning in *Labaye*, the new test is objective (rather than based on subjective judicial interpretations of what a community would tolerate others seeing and doing) because it relies on formal societal recognition of harm as articulated constitutionally and upheld by judges and juries. This move separates the determination of harm from "community values" to become "political values," as if they are conceptually different values. Moreover, the underlying rationale presumes that "harm" is a fixed category rather than a container into which judges can pour meaning in the coming decades.

The new harm-based test is also justified through an appeal to a functionalist view of the role of law in protecting society from harm. Views about the harm that the sexual conduct at issue may produce, however widely held, do not suffice to ground a conviction. This is not to say that social values no longer have a role to play. On the contrary, to ground a finding that acts are indecent, the harm must be shown to be related to a fundamental value reflected in our society's Constitution or similar fundamental laws, like bills of rights, which constitute society's formal recognition that harm of the sort envisaged may be incompatible with its proper functioning. Unlike the community standard of tolerance test, the requirement of formal recognition inspires confidence that the values upheld by judges and jurors are truly those of Canadian society. Autonomy, liberty, equality and human dignity are among these values, yet they are only at issue when they threaten the proper functioning of society (para. 33).

Here we can see that the Court fails to recognize that judges and jurors give content to the sorts of things that ostensibly harm political values and therefore undermine the proper functioning of society. Such reasoning assumes there has been no debate in the literature about whether or not obscenity and indecency cause moral harm (Koppelman 2005) or whether censorship is the approach that ought to be taken in addressing the issue of "evil" ideas (Koppelman 2006). Instead, the Court divorces harm from a focus on direct and attitudinal harm to citizens by shifting the focus towards harm to societal values. Once the Court's theory of harm steps towards affronts to political values, we enter a quasi-authoritarian legal regime in which ideas about autonomy, liberty and equality are fixed; it is only Court who will decide when these values have been harmed in relation to the proper functioning of society. What is absent from judicial consideration is the harm in relation to actual persons in lived contexts because evidence of harm is only required *de facto* and not *de jure*, such that the community's views have been replaced with those of the judiciary acting in the place of the sovereign. Therefore, substantive harms to women's equality or the harm caused to women's freedom to engage in sexual practices by the criminalization of indecency are the other side of a political coin that may rarely be seen under this sort of governmental rationality. The Court has created a kind of moral fusion between "law and order" and the policing of political values through assessment of risky/unruly sexualities (i.e., "dangerous" sex practices). This new approach is further extended to include more than abstract harm to political values that interfered with the proper functioning of society, but also risk of harm to political values that might undermine the proper functioning of society. The Court's use of risk discourse to achieve this objective is problematic given that the purpose of risk analyses are to predict future offending behaviour and little else; the analysis of risk in the service of criminalization is particularly troublesome.

Risks of Harm: The Private, the Public and the Obvious

In aiming to govern sexual danger through risk of harm to political values, the Court inserts a well understood risk discourse of avoidance and reduction measures into its governance strategy. In doing so, the Court commits what Clear and Cadora (2001: 59) have referred to as a kind of category error, in that a risk management strategy is mainly used to predict future offending of prisoners (based on actuarial data). Similar reasoning is now being adopted as a control strategy to criminalize indecent conduct or obscenity on the un-interrogated (and legally unproven) grounds that it poses a *risk of harm* to society's proper functioning rather than actual physical harm or attitudinal harm, which have traditionally been understood as the result of exposure to obscenity and indecency.[1]

However, our research can find no actuarial data on the risk of harm caused by obscenity or indecency on either consenting or non-consenting populations. We are left with a jurisprudential situation in which a court's perception of what *might* cause harm to political values by a given sexual circumstance is a justification for state power. Therefore, where the new *Labaye* rationale seeks evidence from the Crown of a *risk of harm* to establish the *actus reus* of a crime, it represents a potential widening of the net in relation to punishment of the individual in these sorts of cases. In other words, the Court would allow for a possibility of harm to militate criminalization when the consequences of the act could be dire; hence, the Court cites a potential terrorist attack as justification for requiring little in the way of causal probability and allows for the mere *possibility* of such an attack to justify restraint through criminal sanction. The Court does little to explain when sexual action or sexual expression could amount to the same quantum of consequence as terrorism, but its focus on the risk of such a consequence suggests a relaxation of criminal evidentiary standards. While we could ask whether a government ought act in such situations of imputed risk, we can still problematize whether permission for governmental intervention on the basis of high quantum but improbable harm is a sound principle by which to govern obscenity and indecency.

In the context of sexual morality, juridical discourse has shifted in the direction of law and order by enabling more, rather than less, regulation with the expansion of the harm-based test to include risk of harm. In *Butler*, this risk was measured by the abandonment of community standards of tolerance, but the Court also demonstrated a proclivity that such harms included harm to constitutional values enshrined in law; hence degradation and dehumanization as depicted in sexual expression could violate the community standards of tolerance test. The shift to this type of political morality is completed in *Labaye* through the explication of the degree of harm — that harms must damage social cohesion when actions or speech are incompatible with Canadian society. The community standards of tolerance test asked not whether a citizen would engage in a particular kind of sexual behaviour; instead it asked whether as citizens of a liberal society we *ought to tolerate others engaging in that behaviour*. The new harm test transposes what was mainly a jurisdictional test onto the regulation of conduct (Smith 2006: 5). This move illustrates the kind of activism Hudson (2003: 62) describes as a feature of an "authoritarian populism" framework in law and order:

> Neo-liberal economic orthodoxy insists that "markets must decide".... If governments cannot pursue activism in the economic sphere, but nevertheless wish to project themselves as strong, then they must select some other sphere for activism. Crime fulfils this requirement perfectly, fitting the late-modernist mood for fear of strangers, and the late-modernist mode of laying blame for risk on individuals.

The functionality of the harm test may well create sexual "enemies within" from whom the courts will defend "us" in the name of protecting constitutional values. When, as in *Labaye*, "others" are insular and sequestered from proper society, such conduct is permissible, because the "infection" is contained (Jochelson 2009a, 2009b).

The use of *risk of harm* as a factor to substantiate guilt in any case before the Court creates more opportunity for state intervention to criminalize conduct and censor sexually explicit materials. However, because the new test abandons the community standards of tolerance test to determine undue exploitation, replacing it with the more abstract test of risk of harm and harm to individuals *and* society's political values, questions about the negative impact of criminalization and its effects on individuals and communities of interest are minimized. When we protect values rather than people, the context of sexual expression or sexual conduct is utterly lost.

Under the old community standards of tolerance test there remained juridical space for public discussion about direct harm, attitudinal harm and offence to political values. We argue that this discussion has been muted in favour of legal positivism; under the *Butler* test, the Court opened the debate to discuss the kinds of harm that Canadian society might tolerate, and it sought intervener briefs from a variety of affected communities. Such briefs lose vitality under *Labaye*'s faux causality, which prizes social science evidence but also celebrates risk as a justification for criminalization — certainly this provides potential for disapposite reasoning. This is especially troublesome in the contemporary era where governments try to manage risk and promote security at the expense of due process (Hudson 2003).

Pre-*Labaye*, the Canadian courts were provisionally required to weigh evidence of the Canadian community's perspective on these moral questions. The *Labaye* Court now demands evidence of harm and risk of harm (rather than tolerance of particular kinds of materials), but courts are not required as a matter of law to consider the subjective perspective of the community on moral questions having to do with sexually explicit materials and practices. As a result, we are left with a situation where we must rely on the judiciary to seek evidence of harm and risk of harm; this will usually require social science, we are assured by the majority in *Labaye*, but once again, the Court allows that the more extreme the nature of the harm the less evidence need be tendered. We are thus sceptical that triers of fact will seek the factual evidence of harm and will find the causality they seek in the neutral language of social science and risk-based treatises. Worse, obvious affronts might well require less in the way of causality — a matter we discuss below.

Evidence of context, subjectivity and interpretation, for instance, in the form of intervener evidence from multiple-affected communities, has provided courts with powerful factual evidence to support sexual freedom for minority groups in Canada. Intervening evidence of the value of radical sexual conduct in communities of alternative sexualities (for instance, as was the case in *Little Sisters*) proves distracting from the real harm: the promulgation of the infection (the depraved conduct or expression) into society at large. This process achieved some limited success in *Butler*, which problematized a uni-vocal judicial construction of abstracted universal legal principles, particularly when triers of fact are prone to see risk of harm and harm as "moral danger" (Cossman et al. 1997).

In both *Butler* and *Little Sisters*, members of multiple communities, including sexual minorities, presented intervener briefs that the Court considered in its determination of the constitutional justification for the community standards of tolerance test. Once a consideration of the community's viewpoints on tolerance is abandoned and replaced by a more abstract and decontextualized, albeit "objective," exploration of harms and risk of harms, political debate about moral questions is foreclosed. In other words, by abandoning the community standards of tolerance test in favour of a deontological approach to harm, the Court has reduced its own opportunities for seeking input from a range of affected communities to determine whether the sexually explicit materials or acts in question have factual harmful consequences that warrant criminalization. *Labaye* imposes a norm to serve the "proper" functioning of society — a "model of order that is projected onto human conduct" (Bauman 2000: 24). The Court's social order is already free from sexual inequality and the oppression of marginalized sexual minorities, and its aim is to intercede into the field to inoculate society from risks and harms that undermine its proper functioning.

Therefore, the Court constitutes society as one in which liberty and equality exist *a priori* as a sustaining feature. Liberal constitutional values are both *threatened* and *harmed* by obscenity and indecency and therefore disrupt the smooth functioning of a consensual moral order. Rather than seeing inequality and the oppression of sexual minorities as a structural feature of society, wherein the work of the courts is a mechanism for redress, the *Labaye* Court operates as the paternalistic protector of society from those sexual practices it deems risky and harmful. As we illustrate through our discussion of the *Sheikh* decision below, risk can trump both evidenced-based decision-making and sexual freedom in the name of protecting "us" from "them." That the "us" also includes children at risk and other non-consenting populations only makes the approach that much more appealing.

The posited harm test thus becomes another technology of risk in the field of criminal justice. Much like other risk technologies, the risk here is not "regarded as intrinsically real, but as a particular way in which problems are viewed, imagined and dealt with" (Rose, O'Malley and Valverde 2006: 18). In practice, the probabilistic technique in which "large numbers of events" are "sorted into distribution" (18) — i.e., the articulation of risk of harm — is delegated to the analytical contortions of lower courts, with the Supreme Court stating that an "obvious" risk of harm could obviate the need for factual evidence.

In this regard, it appears that in terms of indecency adjudication, the private/public distinction is one aspect which could make the risk of harm sufficient enough to disregard any scientific evidence of risk, other than circumstances. In that regard, the harm-based test draws a boundary around the private sphere whilst widening the boundaries of state intervention in the public sphere, largely on the basis of perceived threats to abstract political values like autonomy, irrespective of any actual harm caused. This is not to say that the private/public divide for the purposes of indecency is new after *Labaye*. What is new is the specifically articulated deployment of risk discourse and the definition of certain public behaviours as risky and therefore presumptive of harm to society's proper functioning. Under the new theory of harm, any citizen walking down the street who encounters a couple engaged in consensual sex has had their liberty value infringed (rather than their *actual* liberty), which, under the new test, causes *harm*. Constructing harm as a threat to political values allows fact finders to insert their "own knowledge" to construct harm. Certainly both *Mara* and *Tremblay* use this kind of assessment in determining whether the community standards of tolerance test for harm was offended, though the discourse penned was less pointed.

Post-*Labaye*, there continues to be a tendency to presume harm on the basis of risk analytics, and this occurs at a cost to evidentiary strictures; moreover, circumstantial evidence operates as a type of causal link in cases of acute affronts to "liberty." For instance, in *R. v. Sheikh* (2008), the accused was caught with a prostitute in the evening in a high school parking lot. Both Sheikh and the woman were visible to the police officers. Because there was a basketball game at the high school, there were people parked in the school's lot and children were potentially in the area, the Court seemed disinclined to consider any evidence as to whether the conduct was harmful. After all, this was public sexuality; the harm was *obvious*:

> The facts are that the Appellant was seated in a reclining position in the driver's seat of his vehicle with his pants at his ankles, his penis was erect and he was in the course of putting a condom on his penis. The context of those acts was that he was accompanied by a woman, he was in a position in his car where he was fully visible to outsiders, the car was located in the middle of the parking lot of a high school, the parking lot was illuminated, there were 65 to 70 cars in the parking lot, it was approximately 8:00 p.m. and there

were many individuals who were attending a basketball game at the high school and who were entering and leaving the parking lot... based on those facts and in those circumstances, expert evidence is not necessary to determine whether there is harm or a significant risk of harm which is incompatible with the proper functioning of society. (*R. v. Sheikh* 2008: paras. 35–36)

Relying on the *Labaye* evidentiary standard, as a "general rule" (para. 32), the Court said that the reference in the *Labaye* decision to consider expert evidence was outside of the context of "obvious cases," where no one could argue that the conduct was incompatible with the proper functioning of society (para. 32). The Court noted that *Labaye* not only contemplated cases where there was no evidence as to nature and degree of harm but where incompatibility of the proper functioning of society was obvious (para. 33). Lastly, citing *R. v. Mohan* [1994], the Court noted that the assistance of expert evidence was required only when it was necessary to appreciate facts due to their technical nature or to form a correct judgment outside the knowledge of ordinary persons (para. 34).

The decision in *Sheikh* accords with a popular understanding of the harm that might be caused to children exposed to sexual activity. Few amongst us would like our children exposed to an erect penis on their way to a basketball game. However, this emerging jurisprudence reifies a world in which criminal indecency is established only through circumstantial evidence. Any need for expert substantiation of harm is dismissed by the *Sheikh* Court in relation to the judge's perception of the obviousness of the harm. Criminal indecency has occurred because the judge said so and it is therefore now a legal fact. No substantiation of harm by virtue of other evidence is necessary. This construction of sexual danger chimes comfortably with a post-9/11 risk-averse society in which popular punitiveness drives crime control policies. However, this same construction of sexual danger, in the context of an adjudication of a *Little Sisters*–style scenario produces different sorts of effects. Now a court could infer risk of harm, or harm, from queer sexually explicit expression created by and for queer communities that depicts stylized violence or degrading and dehumanizing sexual conduct. In other words, these sorts of sexual expression may continue to be the sort of sexually explicit materials deemed worthy of state sanction in a post-*Labaye* world. There is no longer any need for expert or intervening argumentation (i.e., of the kind provided by LEAF and EGALE and others with a political interest in sexual freedom).

The Socially Functional Subject as Abstract Legal Subject

Related to the above construction of harm as risk, is the way a court can constitute its knowledge of that risk. Prior to *Labaye*, in attempting to understand whether obscenity or indecency was established, the Court turned to community standards of tolerance as the indicia. As a court attempted to examine the harms of sexual expression or speech, it was open to disparate voices of social context, either through social science evidence or the political arguments of interveners. The use of stronger risk of harm language, coupled with the abandonment of the community standards test, which allowed for the contextualized voices of sexual minorities and women to be heard as interveners, may pose very real evidentiary issues that are more troubling than the numerous complaints about the amorphous nature of social science evidence. In particular, the appeal to objectivity may obfuscate the voices of the few who may support "questionable" speech or acts, arguing that such expression or activity is liberatory. Certainly, in some intervener briefs in *Little Sisters* such voices were heard and argued that queer sexual expression was a form of political speech that was tolerated, encouraged and beneficial to its own communities. While these voices need not be determinative of adjudication, they may provide powerful context to a court in the midst of adjudication and could lead to censorship and criminalization, especially when risk of harm might result in criminalization. Indeed, the Court has succeeded in removing obscenity and indecency adjudication from the realm of social science and politics.

Benhabib postulates that the abstract, rights-bearing subject is a generalized other: "moral dignity is not what differentiates us from each other, but rather what we, as speaking and rational agents, have in common" (Benhabib 1992: 158–59; D. Young 2008: 15). Young (2008: 36) recently argued that, while the construction of the reasonable person as a tool of analysis in criminal adjudication has traditionally been characterized as type of non-recognitive generalized other, this is not the whole story. Through a rigorous case analysis, Young argues that the reasonable person construct can, and has, come to challenge the "legal subject as generalized other by requiring us to imagine an actual person with concrete characteristics" (36). The result, for Young, is a challenge to "monological approaches" to normative reasoning. Young acknowledges that the recognition of a "concretized other" is ill-defined in terms of how such evidence is admitted into a proceeding and that the concretizing nature of the reasonable person thus remains limited in terms of what "they can reveal about concrete evidence, and more importantly, how that existence might affect normative judgments about an action" (36). Young's contention that contemporary reasonable person jurisprudence provides a counterpoint to the generalized other cannot be achieved through *Labaye*-style reasoning.

The community standards of tolerance test allowed for Young's conception of the concrete other, albeit communally. The intervener evidence in cases such as *Butler* and *Little Sisters*, while not necessarily convincing the

Court of its positions, provided the Court with concrete subjectivities. These briefs helped inform the context of the sexual speech at issue. The *Labaye* decision would silence such voices by asking for causal harm or, in its place, risk of harm to abstract or generalized political values, rather than concrete persons. The risks of speech or acts of a sexual nature are not muted by universalized opinion evidence; indeed, they may well be exacerbated. For example, in *Little Sisters,* some interveners representing queer communities argued for sexual expression rather than for censorship. The *Labaye* decision does not affirm the kind of concrete legal subject Benhabib (1992) envisions or the concretized reasonable person Young endorses. *Labaye* constructs a test based upon the so-called objective universalism of the generalized other. When harm is established through *Labaye*, often because it is "obvious," we lose all sense of difference and we eschew recognition of lived experience, because the new test for harm is grounded firmly in universal objectivity and abstract political values.

This political morality is rooted in harm to political values (equality, autonomy and liberty), harm to society through the promotion of anti-social conduct and harm to individuals participating in the conduct. We call this strategy neoliberal because the Court extends the regulatory apparatus, suggesting that its decision is enhancing freedom through criminalization of dangerous conduct, since it sees risk of harm as a bright line standard for the establishment of guilt. Yet, this has the unfortunate side effect of removing contextual debate from an accused's potential defence arsenal. In other words, where the Court sees liberty, it is actually effecting less freedom. In terms of participation harms, obscenity and indecency jurisprudence has always placed male attitudes front and centre in the rationale for criminalization. Rather than seeing the social conditions that compel women into the sex trade as the kind of inequality against which to inoculate society, the Court sees attitudinal harm to men, and their subsequent behaviour, as what causes the inequality; the participants come to their participation as equal subjects. The new harm reasoning does not take place in a contextual or even evidence-based world view. The notion of community standards of tolerance had potential to allow for the recognition of difference and that sexually explicit materials need to be understood contextually — from the perspective of marginalized communities. Indeed, LEAF in *Little Sisters* recognized this potential along with the possibility of homophobia being imported into the heart of obscenity doctrine (LEAF Factum, *Little Sisters,* 1999: para 30). It may have been, however, that LEAF simply deployed the community standards of tolerance test to its own advantage by attempting to assert the voice of the marginalized community into the legal discourse on obscenity law. Using this sort of political strategy, the case for obscenity or indecency could be aggravated or mitigated by the multi-vocal character of evidence thus leaving the politics of sexuality *open* to debate. Unlikely defenders of "obscene" speech (such as queer special interest groups in *Little Sisters*) might actually problematize the presumption that certain kinds violent sexual expression are harmful to its participants or society as a whole. The effects on political values such as autonomy under the old approach could swing in any direction! If, under the *Labaye* test, jurists calibrate harms based on their own sense of generalized universality, establishing objective harm or risk of harm loses not only context but may work to buttress law and order: being prudent about risk supports constraint. The "I know it when I see it" test for criminal indecency (and obscenity) has returned under the guise of the *Labaye* harm test.

This type of abstract prudential reasoning allows courts to draw conclusions in the absence of lived experiences and recognition of sexual identities (Benhabib 1992; Young 1990; Cossman et al. 1997; Cornell 1991; Benhabib, Cornell and Fraser 1995). Courts may determine the harm of indecency and obscenity without considering the multiple meanings ascribable to speech or acts of a sexual nature. By relying upon the rhetoric of risk and harm, the Court is able to obfuscate deeper issues and cut off debate about conceptions of the good life that challenge its own functionalist view of society and sexual freedom (e.g., do the practices of bondage, domination, submission and masochism, which may couple sex and violence, threaten women's equality?).

Analyses of obscenity jurisprudence have shown that whenever the courts step into the grey area of "moral danger," they have historically been apt to find serious harm to conservative and heterosexual norms, which is always framed as "harm to society." And, rather than police the direct harm caused to individuals through the eroticization of cruelty, courts have tended to police materials that offend attitudes (Cossman et al. 1997).

If it can be agreed that the *Labaye* Court has marshalled an actuarial principle in the context of constituting criminal guilt for the purposes of obscenity or indecency, it has conflated a juridical justification (risk of harm) for government action with the establishment of criminality. Risk becomes a proxy for offence — already a problematized justification for criminalization. Certainly, proponents of offence as a justification for criminalization exist. Such scholars use appeal to issues like equality or identity politics to support criminalization or at least government sanction — they moderate liberty with other pressing values (Langton 1993; Benedet 2001; MacKinnon 1987). However, such scholars do not purport to advance the primacy of liberal objectives, nor do they put all their faith in objective causality as determinative of social harm (unlike the Court in *Labaye*). *Labaye* creates the opportunity for expansive control of crime. Avoidable offence to political values, as construed by a court, can result in criminal sanction. This is neoliberal terrain in that the dictates of liberalism are used to constrain the freedom of the accused, whilst the context of sexually marginalized communities are quieted by the reflexive reliance on risk logic.

What If Harm Was Never a Liberal Construct?

While some argue that *Labaye* represents a principle of "political morality" (as opposed to "sexual morality" or notions of prudishness), which might include potential for a court to recast sex as pleasurable in future cases (Craig 2009), we claim that even on classical liberal terms, *Labaye* fails. If the Court in *Labaye* contends, as they suggest, that the newly constructed test provides the necessary precision to establish criminal guilt in a liberal society, we investigate if the Court has upheld the liberal promise of the *Charter*. We have already established that one way in which the new harm test is illiberal is in its use of risk to limit purported freedoms. Is the harm that the Court has constructed apprised of fidelity to liberalism in other adjudicative contexts?

Certainly, the idea of harm is canonical, and John Stuart Mill's classic formulation is often cited as providing the most basic notion of the principle: "The sole end for which mankind are warranted, individually or collectively, in interfering with the liberty of action of any of their number is... to prevent harm to others" (Mill 1869: para. 9, cited in Smith 2006: 4). Harm is a necessary but not sufficient condition for liberty restraint. Once harm is established, interfering with liberty can only be justified through consequentialism; the benefits of interference must outweigh the costs (Sumner 2004: 33). This basic principle is regarded as a liberal antidote to state paternalism and specifically is used to argue against censorship of pornographic or sexual expression, since such expression has been considered by prominent liberal theorists to be mere slights that ought be tolerated in liberal society (Feinberg 1984, 1985). Clearly, this is not the articulation of harm the Court in *Labaye* has marshalled.

It is important to note that classical liberalism (and even the Supreme Court of Canada itself) view the harm principle in jurisdictional terms rather than as an element in the *actus reus* of a crime. The harm principle does not moralize about the ethics of regulation of an individual in a particular case (Smith 2006: 5). In the context of "psychic" or "communal" harms, such as anti-social attitudinal changes and unwanted deprivations of autonomy, these sorts of "intangible" harms (which are *Labaye*-style harms) are conceptualized as not simply justifications for providing a government with the jurisdiction to regulate. In other words the construction of the harm principle in the traditional sense usually justifies government intrusion into the lives of the citizen rather than the construction of criminal guilt. If the *Labaye* Court is seeking to marshal a harm principle in order to constitute criminal guilt for the purposes of obscenity of indecency, it has indeed stepped outside of classical liberal rationales for state intervention and into new governance territory. This is territory where easily avoidable offence can result in criminalization. This is perhaps neoliberal terrain in that the dictates of liberalism are used to constrain the freedom of the accused, whilst the context of sexually marginalized communities are quieted by the faux appeal to objective establishment of the risk of harm.

Conclusion

In *Labaye*, the Supreme Court of Canada has reified a harm-based test that establishes the *actus reus* of an indecency- or obscenity-based offence on the basis of harm to society, as well as risk of harm to society. The threats include damage to human attitudes and political values. That legally imputed risk can establish the *actus reus* of an offence creates *ex post facto* guilt in some cases, especially where an accused could never be aware that their conduct was capable of changing attitudes or affronting political values. This is in itself a jurisprudential turn that not only results in a novel construction of guilt but creates lacunae in the causal requirements for harm — relaxation of evidentiary strictures when harms are obvious to the trier. The price paid for such a jurisprudential turn is more than discursive — it serves the traditional functionality of obscenity and indecency law and the contortions used to justify criminalizing moral harm.

In the context of obscenity and indecency, the Court is most interested in the proper functioning of society, which is served through criminalizing sexual practices that interfere with the constitutionally enshrined political values (autonomy, liberty and perhaps equality). Presumed threats to constitutional values is the new *Hicklin* moral standard, despite the Court's efforts to distance political morality from subjective moral views: "Canadian law on indecent acts, from it's origins in the English common law, has been firmly anchored in societal rather than purely moral concerns. For example, in the early case of *R. v. Hicklin*, Cockburn, C.J. stated that the test for obscenity was whether the material would tend to deprave and corrupt other members of society" (*R. v. Labaye* 2005: para. 15). For the *Labaye* Court, the problem with *Hicklin* was that it was a subjective test applied unevenly by judges and jurors using their own value judgments. Later the test shifted, asking judges and jurors to consider community values in determining harm to society. Again, the *Labaye* Court is dissatisfied with this approach because it continues to allow judges and jurors to interpose their own subjective beliefs about would others might tolerate: "The result was that despite its superficial objectivity, the community standard of tolerance test remained highly subjective in application" (para. 18). It is only the shift towards a harm-based test that begins to satisfy the *Labaye* Court.

By teasing out the thread of harm and risk of harm, the language of the rationality underpinning obscenity and indecency jurisprudence shifts away from grounding power within the subjectivity of the Canadian community (albeit as perceived by judges and jurors) towards a more abstracted rationality, which the Court argues is more *objective* because "harm or significant risk of harm is easier to prove than a community standard" (para. 24). Thus, the Court marches towards pseudo-scientificity and objectivity in its logic and effort to ground harm in social norms in order to maintain social order. The Court may not be able to list specific incidences of obscenity and indecency, but they understand that risk of harm can justify criminalization when they see it. The Court has thus embraced a neo-Hicklenesque principle for obscenity and indecency under the guise of its harm-based test.

Note

1. "Risk of harm" as a governmental technology has been at play in lower court decisions for some time (see Valverde 1999). *R. v. Jacobs* (1996) was a case where the Ontario Court of Appeal agreed with the concept that a harm-based test ought to apply to public indecency (in the context of bare breasts in public), but found that the quantum of harm contemplated by the Crown was not made out on the facts of the case (1996: para. 23):

    > In my opinion, there is no evidence of harm that is more than grossly speculative. All that the trial judge had before him was some evidence indicating specific individuals' lack of acceptance of the appellant's choice of clothing. There was nothing degrading or dehumanizing in what the appellant did. The scope of her activity was limited and was entirely non-commercial. No one who was offended was forced to continue looking at her. I cannot conclude that what the appellant did exceeded the community standard of tolerance when all of the relevant circumstances are taken into account. It follows that what the appellant did on July 19, 1991 did not constitute an indecent act.

Chapter Four

Challenges to Sex Laws Post-*Labaye*

Indecency and Prostitution

The main tension in feminist debates in the area of indecency and prostitution centres on the issue of decriminalization. Driven by a vocal contingent of sex trade workers, sometimes referred to as people working in the sex industry, there has been a call in some feminist circles for a "world-wide decriminalization of the sex industry" (Delacoste and Alexander 1988; van der Meulen and Durisin 2008). These arguments in favour of decriminalization stand in sharp contrast to a variant of what is sometimes called a "radical feminist approach" (which in previous chapters we have equated with an anti-pornography feminist position), adopted in countries like Iceland and Sweden, where criminalization of the sex trade has been stepped up, with an enhanced punishment scheme in recent years. This approach to law reform, which is a kind of censorship of the sex trade, is problematized by anti-criminalization activists for having too much in common with paternalistic nineteenth-century anti-prostitution moral reformers who sought to protect women and children from the "wiles of the procurer" (i.e., working-class men) (van der Meulen and Durisin 2008: 291; McLaren 1985: 136; Valverde 1991). According to van der Meulen and Durisin (2008: 291):

> Often couched in the language of the nineteenth-century abolitionists and the early moral reformers, this group has been highly successful in influencing prostitution policy both in Canada and internationally. Contemporary radical feminist theorizing on women's social and sexual subjugation has often conceptualized women's secondary status in relation to women's sexual subordination to men. Radical feminists have translated this ideological positioning into a clearly defined anti-prostitution stance, which has been, and continues to be, influential in informing public policy responses to prostitution-related issues. Within radical feminist debates on sex work, there has traditionally been a lack of focus on sex worker agency and, instead, an understanding that all sex workers are victims.

In contrast to the nineteenth-century concern with "moral corruption," contemporary radical feminists want to deploy the power of the law to reverse "women's secondary status in relation to women's sexual subordination to men" (van der Meulen and Durisin 2008: 291). Using the law as a means of promoting women's equality, radical feminists who advocate for the criminalization of sex work to protect women are joined by those feminists such as Waltman (2010) who advocate the use of censorship of pornography to promote women's equality. Both of these political approaches to law are easily accommodated by the harms-based configuration of obscenity and indecency law.

Those who advocate the decriminalization of prostitution view people working in the sex trade as active participants in a multivalent and sophisticated sex industry characterized not by violence and exploitation but by unfair and unsafe labour practices (Chapkis 1998; Nussbaum 1999; Lowman 1998, 2000; O'Connell Davidson 1998; Sanders 2005; van der Meulen and Durisin 2008: 292). In many regards, the tension between anti-prostitution radical feminists and pro-regulation sex trade workers and advocates mirrors the tension between anti-pornography radical feminists (MacKinnon 1987; Benedet 2001; Kendall 2004a, 2004b; Waltman 2010) and anti-censorship feminists, who are much more sceptical of the use of obscenity law to promote women's equality (Valverde 1999; Cossman 1997; Gotell 1997; Ross 1997; Bell 1997). Decriminalization advocates challenge the assumption by radical feminists that sex trade workers are victims of patriarchy and focus instead on "sex worker agency" and, like the anti-censorship feminists discussed above, they problematize the radical feminist assumption that all sex trade work is exploitative and violent (van der Meulen and Durisin 2008; Farley 1998). In that regard, the anti-prostitution position is criticized for its "tendency to universalize the experiences of prostitution by taking worst case scenarios to be representative of all sex work" (Van der Meulen and Durisin 2008; Shaver 1988; Weitzer 2005). Van der Meulen and Durisin, both sex trade workers themselves, advocate the regulatory model currently in place in New Zealand because it puts sex workers' rights at the forefront to effectively enhance the health, safety and labour market position of women (2008: 291). Nevertheless, the pro-criminalization perspective dominates the political agenda. which is no surprise given the current law and order climate in Canada. According to van der Meulen and Durisin (2008: 293):

> Despite critique and research to the contrary, the radical feminist perspective has been able to maintain legitimacy among some politicians in Canada. Indeed, the Conservative Party member of the recent Subcommittee on Solicitation Laws Review... expressed

support for the victimization perspective on sex work, stating that "the most realistic, compassionate and responsible approach to dealing with prostitution begins by viewing most prostitutes as victims." While there is a large body of research demonstrating the ineffectiveness of, and harms caused by, Canada's prostitution laws, there is a considerable reluctance on the part of politicians to reform the *Criminal Code*. The hesitation to advocate for decriminalization points to an unwillingness to accept an analysis that has developed from sex workers themselves—one that advocates an understanding of sex work as a form of labour and a framing of sex work issues within health, human, and labour rights discourses.

The paternalistic, victim-based approach has been challenged using a harms-based approach to prostitution, in an effort to decriminalize indoor prostitution, which makes up 80 to 90 percent of sex trade work in Canada (Hangar and Maloney 2006; Lewis and Maticka-Tyndale 2000).

In this chapter, we discuss the link established between the "bawdy house" provision of the *Criminal Code* and the harm test defined by the *Labaye* Court. Usually the decision to lay a bawdy house charge is because the Crown has less confidence in its ability to prove "prostitution" or that sexual practices were exchanged for money. The Crown may believe it can secure a conviction by meeting the harm test set out in *Labaye* to establish the "indecency" component. In other words, in those cases where the sex work involves massage parlours, stripping and lap-dancing or escort services, the Crown could try and establish indecency through the harm test of *Labaye* for a conviction, thereby meeting at least one of the crucial circumstances for establishing the *actus reus* of the criminal offence of keeping a common bawdy house. That said, were the Crown able to demonstrate that money exchanged hands between adults for the purposes of sexual services, prostitution would be established, and this alone could meet one of the circumstances for a bawdy house offence. Stated more simply, a bawdy house conviction can be secured either by proving prostitution *or* indecency (which is now established through the harm-based test set out in *Labaye*).

This dual approach to the criminalization of sexual conduct of various sorts (not all of which involve sexual intercourse) has created significant challenges for those who seek to decriminalize prostitution. Reform of the prostitution/bawdy house scheme require changes to both sections of the *Criminal Code*. However, a political strategy could leapfrog the legislative process, forcing government to undertake law reform if the laws are struck down. Given the issues discussed in respect of the *Labaye* harm principle in the last chapter, certain political approaches that have recently emerged in Canada might result in unintended consequences, both for Canadians and sex workers.

Some argue that the *Labaye* harm test is a "victory for women's equality" because they view the test as a shift from sexual morality to political morality — the latter being apprised of equality rights and thusly the "correct" sort of politics for courts to consider (Craig 2008: 350, footnote 18). Of course, feminist politics is not without moral foundations. Where some see what has been described as a shift towards an "illiberal" use of the harm principle (Smith 2006), others see the use of a harms-based test as a victory because the courts *may* now marshal the political value of harm (to equality, autonomy etc.) to promote the proper functioning of society. This is despite the fact that the technology for intervention remains Hicklinesque. We argue that the harms-based test has been re-branded in feminist friendly terms.

The positive view of the *Labaye* decision is similar to the optimistic reading of *Butler* when it was declared to be a feminist victory (MacKinnon 1993; Scales 1994). However, as we have noted, a harms-based calculus allows for accommodation of multiple objectives, which may be contradictory and/or ambiguous. For example, a court's determination that a sexual act in public is indecent meets a harm threshold because a judge sees the behaviour as incompatible with society's proper functioning. This calculus is aimed at protecting the passerby from harm, rather than protecting women's equality interests. On the other hand, a radical feminist might see the state as preventing harm to women's equality interests when it criminalizes conduct that is connected to street prostitution. Nevertheless, the result may be an interlocking of political interests: the court's philosophy sees its functionalism as premised on an original position of formal equality, while the radical feminist approach would assume the opposite. Because the harms-based approach is open-ended, it accommodates a plurality of political affinities and therefore produces contradictions.

The arguments in favour of and against prostitution as a criminalizable enterprise have been well articulated in the literature (Hangar and Mahoney 2006; Pivot Legal Society 2004; Gorkoff and Runner 2003; Shaver 1988). Recently, certain provisions of the *Criminal Code* have been challenged in order to improve the working conditions of sex trade workers (see *Bedford v. Canada* 2010). Craig (2008) argues that the *Labaye* harm principle can be used to decriminalize prostitution on the grounds that the state interferes with women's liberty when the law undermines women's sexual pleasure (articulated in feminist terms as harm to women's pursuit of sexual pleasure, which promotes women's self-determination and therefore equality). Both approaches are informed by the notion that these incremental law reforms promote women's equality. In Craig's view, the harm principle can be deployed to achieve feminist-friendly law reform. This repeats the strategy used by LEAF in the *Little Sister* case because it marshals liberalism to achieve feminist political goals. LEAF used the liberal notion of "freedom of expression" to defend queer erotica; now political activists use harm to "liberty" to argue in favour of protecting women against criminalization of prostitution. The harm that the *Labaye* court attempts to prevent is not aimed at protecting women as an equality-seeking group, but rather is aimed at protecting society as a whole (of which women are members!).

In Canada, the anti-prostitution laws (communicating for the purposes of prostitution, pimping and operating a common bawdy house) were challenged in an Ontario court by *cause célèbre* dominatrix Terri-Jean Bedford and two former prostitutes, Valerie Scott and Amy Lebovitchon, on the grounds that they compel women to work without protection and in the streets, where they are subject to increased violence and victimization. In September 2010, Justice Himel of the Ontario Superior Court struck down those laws and gave the government thirty days to respond. At the time of writing, the case is before the Ontario Court of Appeal. According to Kirk Makin, justice reporter for the *Globe and Mail*, Himel's 131-page judgment, which took a year to write, "pointed at evidence that established violence against sex workers is endemic — from a string of gruesome serial killings by Vancouver pig farmer Robert Pickton, to a rash of missing prostitutes in Alberta and frequent violence against sex trade workers in the Atlantic region" (Makin 2010). Himel's decision focused directly on *harm*, caused this time by the government through law: "'By increasing the risk of harm to street prostitutes, the communicating law is simply too high a price to pay for the alleviation of social nuisance,' she said. 'I find that the danger faced by prostitutes greatly outweighs any harm which may be faced by the public'" (Makin 2010). Scott, Lebovitchon and Bedford seek a similar regulatory regime to that adopted in New Zealand, Germany and Australia, which "includes workers' compensation, health standards and inclusion in the country's income-tax scheme. 'We don't have to worry about being raped or robbed or murdered,' [Scott] said" (Makin 2010).

On the other hand, Craig (2008, 2009) suggests that the *Labaye* harm test should be imported into the definition of prostitution, so that you would only arrest people who were engaged in prostitution-related offences that were "harmful," using the *Labaye* categories of harm (harm to the passerby etc.). Rather than focus on the commercial sexual nature of the conduct, the focus shifts towards more abstract considerations of harm to political values, including equality. This harms-based analysis asks the courts to consider whether a sexual act is harmful by determining if the functioning of society at large is obstructed. Now we see a feminist rationality deployed in Durkheimian terms to justify the use of power. However, this rationality might also convert prostitution that was otherwise legal (i.e., because the Crown could not prove that a sexual transaction for money occurred) into an illegal act by finding the activity in question to be "harmful" sexual activity.

Once the activity becomes harmful in legal terms, it is also legally indecent. Thus, this strategy uses a particular harm rationale to re-define indecency in feminist terms.

Regardless if one adopts the Bedford approach, which focuses on harm to the sex trade worker, or the approach advanced by Craig (2008, 2009), both seek to drop those elements of the prostitution legal framework that harm women in the ways that each defines as harm (harm to equality, harm to security of the person, harm to liberty, etc.). In this regard, both of the arguments adopt a *Labaye*-style rationality for a more laissez-faire state in which sex trade workers are not prosecuted unless their activities cause "social nuisance," which the courts have understood as harm to other people's liberty interests. The social nuisance elements of the street trade are what each have in mind as causing harm.

Coupling Prostitution and Indecency:
The Legal Meaning of Prostitution

The link between prostitution and indecency has always been murky, which the *Criminal Code* maintains through a series of complex provisions that criminalize the conduct of those who engage in the sex trade. For example, section 210 of the *Code* creates offences for those who keep or in some capacity engage with "bawdy houses" — which in turn are defined as houses kept for indecency or prostitution (s.197). Section 213 addresses communicating for the purposes of prostitution and criminalizes certain kinds of social nuisance that street prostitution might inure. Sections 211 and 212 deal respectively with transporting individuals to a bawdy house and procuring prostitution. The result is a hodgepodge of prohibitions that essentially criminalize virtually all behaviour associated with the sex trade. In respect of the bawdy house offences, the *Code* provides a regime whereby the Crown can establish the criminal circumstances of the offence by demonstrating that the behaviour in question was either indecent or an act of prostitution.

A harm-based rationale for dealing with sexual conduct is one for which anti-criminalization advocates have argued since the Supreme Court of Canada ruled in *Prostitution Reference* in 1990. This was a constitutional question taken to the Supreme Court by the Lieutenant Governor in Council of Manitoba to determine whether two sections of the *Criminal Code* ("communications in public for the purpose of prostitution" and "keeping of common bawdy houses") violated the freedom of expression guarantee under s. 2(b) of the *Charter*. In large part, advocates for the decriminalization of prostitution rely on the work of the 2006 Standing Committee on Justice and Human Rights, which noted that "the social and legal framework pertaining to adult prostitution does not effectively prevent and address prostitution or the exploitation and abuse... or harms to communities"

(Hanger and Maloney 2006: 86). Indeed, arguments for decriminalization and regulation have had some legislative and empirical support since the Fraser Report (1985). These studies found that the criminal regulation of prostitution in Canada creates secrecy and isolation for Canada's sex trade workers, thus making the workers more susceptible to violence (Lowman 2000; Pivot Legal Society 2004). Thus, some scholars argue passionately that the harm-based approach towards indecency in *Labaye* should be transposed into the definition for prostitution. This re-definition would then be a means of understanding the harms caused to women by the criminalization of sex work in the context of the array of prostitution-related offences. Thus, the offence of communicating for the purposes of prostitution would require that the Crown demonstrate harm, using the *Labaye* test (Craig 2008: 342–46). However, this understanding of harm is a sociological feminist one rather than a legal one. The Court in *Labaye* is concerned largely with the maintenance of social order and understands harm only in that functionalist manner. Feminist anti-criminalization advocates understand laws in relation to harm to women rather than harm to the proper functioning of society (MacKinnon 1987; Benedet 2001).

In part, arguments about the harms of the legal regime governing prostitution rely on the myth that prostitution itself is legal, which was first articulated in the *Prostitution Reference* (1990). The idea is based, in part, on the famous passage from the *Reference*, in which the majority wrote: "The fact that the sale of sex for money is not a criminal act under Canadian law does not mean that Parliament must refrain from using the criminal law to express society's disapprobation of street solicitation." The majority here is recognizing that while the sale of sex for money is not itself a crime, the circuitous route of criminalizing communicating for the purposes of affecting that sale is within the constitutional purview of government. In other words, government can indirectly criminalize what it deems to be immoral conduct. The constitution does not limit indirect sanctions as a principle of fundamental justice (*Prostitution Reference* 1990). Yet, this reasoning by the Court is fictitious. In a legislative scheme where communicating for the sale of sex, keeping, working, visiting or transporting a person to a bawdy house which sells sex, and procuring the sale of sex are all criminalized, and where public indecency (when it is deemed "harmful") is criminalized, the claim that prostitution has never been illegal is untenable. Though the scheme is clearly clumsy and, in the case of indecency-based offences, contingent on a finding of harm to the proper functioning of society, the familiar refrain that prostitution is legal in Canada must be contextualized. Clearly Canadian society, Parliament, and the courts do not hold criminal the mere identification of a person as a prostitute, but the *Code* goes to great lengths to repress a large swath of sex worker activities because these activities are considered a "social nuisance." In other words, Parliament was concerned with preventing the social problems it constructs in respect of people engaging in the sex trade. While the sale of sex for money is standing alone *legal*, in combination with certain circumstances, it becomes illegal. In other words, it is not illegal to identify as a prostitute on your Facebook page, but when you sell sex inside a house you will have committed an offence under the bawdy house prohibitions. In the same way, the *Criminal Code* does not prevent anyone from identifying as a "murderer," but criminalizes any and all acts that are associated with the intentional or negligent infliction of physical harm resulting in death or serious injury. Put another way, the *Code* usually concerns itself with criminal acts as opposed to criminal thoughts. The *Code* does not per se criminalize the act of selling sex alone, but rather prohibits that act in certain circumstances (such as in a bawdy house). Nonetheless, the act of selling sex remains a vital part of the criminal act in such offences.

Recent Ontario court decisions maintain that the definition of prostitution remains essentially the sale of sexual services for money (*R. v. Ponomarev* 2007). Indeed, the Supreme Court of Canada, according to Justice Lamer's concurring reasons in the *Prostitution Reference*, support this common sense definition:

> Prostitution for example has been defined as the offering by a person of his or her body for lewdness for payment in return: see *R. v. Lantay*, [1966] 3 C.C.C. 270 (Ont. C.A.), adopting the English position in *R. v. De Munck*, [1918] 1 K.B. 635 (C.C.A.). It seems to me that there is little dispute as to the basic definition of prostitution, that being the exchange of sexual services of one person in return for payment by another. (*Prostitution Reference* 1990: 41)

Thus, the bawdy house prohibitions can be triggered by acts of indecency (which is defined by *Labaye*) or by acts of prostitution (defined in both *Prostitution Reference* and recently in cases such as *R. v. Pomeranov* (2007) as the sale of sexual services for money). Any argument that the meaning of prostitution is now to be defined as when *Labaye*-style harm occurs is a hopeful activist fiction.

In lower court cases, where the notions of indecency and prostitution are often confused, judges manage to make separate findings regarding *Labaye* harm and prostitution. For instance, in *R. v. Ponomarev* (2007), where an accused faced bawdy house charges due to operating a massage parlour, Studio 176, the judge considered the *Labaye* test and determined that the acts of masturbation occurred in private, between consenting adults, without the threat of fear and were sequestered from residential areas. The case was the result of a police sting operation that targeted the massage parlour, located in an industrial strip mall in the City of Vaughn, Ontario, in 2003. The judge concluded, "When I apply the test that is set out by the Supreme

Court of Canada [in *Labaye*] in these facts, I am not satisfied that the Crown has met its obligation to prove beyond a reasonable doubt that there was 'the practice of acts of indecency'" (*R. v. Ponomarev* 2007: paras. 29–30). Further, the Court was unconvinced that the masturbation in question "constitute[d] acts of sexual gratification in return for the payment of money," principally because the masturbation was not negotiated for as part of the massage: "The payment of money as I have found it was for a full body massage. The act of masturbation was optional, at no additional fee" (para. 34).[1] In the absence of indecency or prostitution, the Court would not uphold the bawdy house charge. Perhaps most interestingly, the judge was uncertain that the acts of masturbation in this case even constituted sex:

> One only needs to look to the conduct of a certain president of the United States and the response to activity that he participated in to wonder whether or not the act of masturbation is indeed in all circumstances a sexual act. (para. 34)

It is interesting to note that male sexual pleasure in this context falls outside of the ambit of law.

In the context of BDSM establishments, the Ontario courts have reached different conclusions. In *R. v. Bedford* (2000), the Court of Appeal considered whether a home that functioned as a sex dungeon, in which some clients were involved in BDSM as well as cock and ball and anus stimulation, was indeed a "bawdy house" for the purposes of prostitution (the issue of indecency was disposed of at trial). While the defence attempted to argue that what the clients were paying for were "games of domination and power" and that the genital stimulation was merely incidental,[2] the Court of Appeal responded as follows, relying on the testimony of sex trade employee Princess:

> While Princess did testify that manual masturbation by the appellant's employees was not permitted, she also testified that: (i) she inserted her finger or a dildo into the client's anus; (ii) she squeezed or pinched client's testicles while they masturbated in order to help them maintain erection; and (iii) she had seen the appellant and other employees doing the same. There was also the fact that a number of dildos were on display and that there was a protocol for cleaning them after use. The dildos were sheathed in condoms for health purposes when in use. This is compelling circumstantial evidence that dildos were part and parcel of the services rendered on the premises and supports the conclusion that genital touching was habitual and frequent and not merely incidental. (*R. v. Bedford* 2000: para. 30)

The discussion of these two cases demonstrates that courts are happy to give meaning to the term prostitution as sexual acts done in exchange for money, where the sexual nature of the act is determined objectively, understood in legal terms as a reasonable person test. Moreover, in *R. v. Bedford* (2000) the Appellate Court imported the test for the meaning of "sexual" from the sexual assault jurisprudence:

> In *R v. Chase* (1987), 37 C.C.C. (3d) 97 (S.C.C.), relied upon by both parties on this issue, the Supreme Court of Canada ruled that the term "sexual" (in the context of "sexual" assault) is to be interpreted looking at all the circumstances.... It is hard to imagine that a reasonable person observing the erotica sessions as described by Princess would not regard them as "sexual," even accepting that such sessions may have been designed to humiliate or degrade the client. (paras 28 and 29)

Both *Ponomarev* (2007) and *Bedford* (2000) indicate that courts are willing to constitute the word "sexual" from the perspective of a "reasonable" third party to establish running a common bawdy house for the purposes of prostitution. Determining whether something is *sexual* is not dissimilar from the Court's rationale in *Labaye*, where the Court argued that obscenity and indecency can be established through an objective harm test. That is, they ask themselves whether a reasonable third party would consider the sexual acts in question harmful to the proper functioning of society. In the examples of both *Ponomarev* and *Bedford*, it is possible to see that the judge puts *himself* in the position of experiencing the sexual conduct to determine whether the criminal threshold has been met. The judge's determination in *Ponomarev* is apprised of his own beliefs, with the result that the happy-ending massage is not deemed to be criminal, whereas in *Bedford*, BDSM sex in a dungeon is criminalized. In both cases, money was exchanged for a sexual service, and yet the only sexual service proscribed is the one to which, apparently, the judge could not relate. Alan Young, Bedford's lawyer in this case, has described this kind of reasoning in similar terms to the ones we are describing, as an emotional response on the part of the judiciary. Young (2008: 215) describes a criminal court which draws a line between "tolerable" and "criminal" behaviour on the basis of "moral assessment of profane bodily functions." In his analysis of the decision, Young notes the revulsion that underscored the judge's decision:

> [The] evidence presented was initially entertaining, it ultimately began to progress to the bizarre and ultimately disgusting. (*R. v. Bedford* transcript of evidence, as cited in Young 2008: 215)

This illustrates beautifully the manner in which psychological reactions to practices are transformed into the legal language of harm. This sort of faux "objective" test is also inscribed by the *Labaye* court through an appeal to abstract political harm (which the Court in *Labaye* claims is an "objective" test) and risks the same sort of "I know it when I see it" ethic of the *Hicklin* court.

Recent Challenges

Following Terri-Jean Bedford's conviction in *R. v. Bedford* (1998, 2000), both she and Toronto lawyer Alan Young challenged the constitutionality of bawdy house and solicitation laws (*Bedford v. Canada* 2010). The Supreme Court of Canada has, in the *Prostitution Reference*, already dismissed constitutional challenges to the solicitation laws and bawdy house prohibitions on the basis that Parliament was within its constitutional jurisdiction to turn its mind to such matters and that the terms prostitution and indecent were not vague because they provided sufficient guidelines for legal debate. Nonetheless, the new challenges to these laws stem from the concerns voiced by those in the anti-criminalization movement over the past decades. They argue that these laws create unsafe working conditions for sex trade workers, limit the economic liberty of these workers, violate their freedom of expression and drive the sex trade onto the streets instead of the workplace, where better safety screening could occur. According to Young (2008: 213):

> What often goes unrecognized is that the daily existence of the sex trade worker on the street is defined by assault and psychological terror. Due to the legal marginalization and stigmatization of sex work, this violence is simply ignored, or routinely addressed with utter indifference by all public officials.

In short, the litigants assert that the laws deny sex workers their right to life, liberty and security of the person under s.7 of the *Charter*. This section of the *Charter* not only protects life, liberty and security of the person but also provides procedural protections to citizens, most saliently in that a law which denies one of these rights cannot be arbitrary or grossly disproportionate in terms of its negative effects on accused persons in light of the objective of protecting them from harm (*R. v. Caine/Malmo-Levine* 2003). Furthermore, deprivations of section 7 rights cannot extend to more activities than are necessary to achieve their objectives, known in the law as "overbreadth" (*R. v. Caine/Malmo-Levine* 2003).

The threshold issue the Court had to face in the case before the Ontario Superior Court (*Bedford v. Canada* 2010) was the Supreme Court's ruling in the *Prostitution Reference*, which seemed to validate the constitutionality of some of the prostitution provisions of the *Code*. In *Bedford* (2010), the Court rejected the Supreme Court's established precedent by asserting:

The Prostitution Reference ought to be revisited given the breadth of evidence that has been gathered over the course of the intervening twenty years. Furthermore, it may be that the social, political, and economic assumptions underlying the Prostitution Reference are no longer valid today. Indeed, several western democracies have made legal reforms decriminalizing prostitution to varying degrees. As well, the type of expression at issue in this case is different from that considered in the Prostitution Reference. Here, the expression at issue is that which would allow prostitutes to screen potential clients for a propensity for violence. I conclude, therefore, that it is appropriate in this case to decide these issues based upon the voluminous record before me. As will become evident following a review of the evidence filed by the parties, there is a substantial amount of research that was not before the Supreme Court in 1990. (83)

The arguments presented in *Bedford v. Canada* (2010) rested on Young's assessment of "the illogical and sinister arbitrariness of the law" (2008: 213). In particular, the law "proclaims the act of prostitution to be legal and yet in the same breath takes away every legal option for securing this work in a safe and secure manner" (213). Furthermore, Young argues that in its totality, the law creates dangerous working conditions for sex trade workers:

Section 213 (1)(c) of the Criminal Code prohibits the acts of communicating for the purpose of prostitution, so it is actually illegal to do any rudimentary screening of customers before entering their cars. Section 212(1)(j) prohibits the act of living on the avails (i.e., earnings) of prostitution and, despite this provision's mistaken association with the insidious act of pimping, this provision does not require proof of any parasitic or exploitive relationship (*R. v. Barrow*, 2001). So it is actually illegal for anyone to work for a prostitute even when this employment is legitimately required for the personal security of the sex trade worker. Finally, s. 210 prohibits the act of keeping a bawdy house on a habitual and frequent basis so, despite the obvious dangers of the street trade the law actually makes it illegal to move into a more secure and safe indoor setting. The bottom line is that it is incoherent for the courts to assert that we prohibit "communication in a public place for the purposes of prostitution" on the basis of combating street nuisance and then turn around and prevent those who are allegedly communicating from moving their business from the streets into a safer, indoor location. (2008: 213)

In part, the impetus for these challenges stem from more recent Parliamentary studies that delineate the acute dangers associated with the sex trade. Using over fifty affidavits from sex trade workers, the applicants seek to establish that Canada's sex trade laws contribute to the violence experienced by women, who disproportionately make up the population of sex trade workers in Canada, which is harmful in liberal legal terms.

The Decision in *Bedford v. Canada* (2010)

The decision by Justice Himel provides a detailed assessment of the prostitution scheme under the *Code*. While the decision is incredibly complex, the rationale for the court's decision that the legislative scheme is unconstitutional included acceptance of the notion that prostitutes face increased safety risks where they are precluded from operating indoors with other people present and from taking steps to screen their clients, which deprives sex trade workers of their right to security of the person under the *Charter*. Ironically, the "living off the avails" provision was intended by Parliament to prevent the exploitation of prostitutes by pimps. This section was deemed arbitrary by Justice Himel because it effectively exposes prostitutes to *greater harm* than they otherwise would face under a different legal regime. Neither the "communicating" nor the "bawdy house" provisions were arbitrary because both were deemed to be connected to the government's objective of controlling public nuisances. However, acting in tandem, the provisions were seen as arbitrary. According to the court, the "living off the avails" and "bawdy house" provisions covered broader circumstances than necessary to achieve their objective of controlling nuisance. This came at a great cost to the safety of sex trade workers. Further, the Court found that the effects of the impugned provisions were disproportionate to their purposes. The "communicating" provision violated the prostitutes' rights to free expression and was not a reasonable limit on such freedom, as it prohibited communications other than simply those contributing to social nuisance. The danger to prostitutes and their exposure to violence was undeniable on the evidence and this outweighed any societal interest posited by the Crown (see paras. 84–506). Justice Himel proceeded to suspend the declaration of invalidity of these provisions for a short period of time:

> I am mindful of the fact that legislating in response to prostitution raises difficult, contentious, and serious policy issues and that it is for Parliament to fashion corrective legislation. This decision does not preclude such a response from Parliament. It is my view that in the meantime, these unconstitutional provisions should be of no force and effect, particularly given the seriousness of the Charter violations. However, I also recognize that a consequence of this

decision may be that unlicensed brothels may be operated and in a way that may not be in the public interest. It is legitimate for government to study, consult and determine how to best address this issue. In light of this, I have determined that a stay of my decision for up to 30 days should be granted to enable the parties to make fuller submissions to me on this question or to seek an order for a stay of my judgment. (para. 539)

Justice Himel pointed out that in the 1990 *Prostitution Reference* the Supreme Court was mainly concerned with the nuisance-based harms of prostitution. A detailed rereading of the Supreme Court decision reveals broader social concerns. The majority of the Supreme Court in that case found that though the sex trade criminal provisions might not be the most effective way of addressing the social harms of prostitution, such a response was a reasonable limit on the freedom of sex trade workers under s.1 of the *Charter*. In particular, the majority noted the following in respect of the harms that Parliament was redressing with the solicitation laws:

> The provision is meant to address solicitation in public places and, to that end, seeks to eradicate the various forms of social nuisance arising from the public display of the sale of sex. My colleague Lamer J. finds that s. 195.1(1)(*c*) is truly directed towards curbing the exposure of prostitution and related violence, drugs and crime to potentially vulnerable young people, and towards eliminating the victimization and economic disadvantage that prostitution, and especially street soliciting, represents for women. I do not share the view that the legislative objective can be characterized so broadly. In prohibiting sales of sexual services in public, the legislation does not attempt, at least in any direct manner, to address the exploitation, degradation and subordination of women that are part of the contemporary reality of prostitution. Rather, in my view, the legislation is aimed at taking solicitation for the purposes of prostitution off the streets and out of public view. (*Prostitution Reference* 1990: 15)

This passage encapsulates two ideas. First, it is an indication that the prevention of criminal nuisance through solicitation laws is a viable constitutional objective. Second, it is a tacit admission that sex trade regulation, *outside* of the solicitation context (i.e., in the bawdy house context), is directed towards preventing the exploitation, degradation and subordination of women. That is, ultimately the prevention of criminal nuisance *and* preventing degradation, exploitation and subordination of women are laudable criminal objectives, which through various provisions, could be competently legislated by government — the purported harms permitted government jurisdiction in these arenas. Here, the Court is merging a principle of *offence* and a principle of *harm* to essentially articulate what would become the content of the *Labaye* harm test, though in this case the Court used its "harm principle" to justify criminal jurisdiction. As discussed earlier, the harm principle has typically been limited to giving government permission to legislate in an area, not necessarily to criminalizing conduct in an individual case. It is an odd judicial turn that fifteen years later, in *Labaye*, a differently constituted court used the same principle to regulate sexual conduct by positing that indecency prohibitions require one of the following harms (which include "mere offences"): affronts to liberty (criminal nuisance), attitudinal predisposition to anti-social viewpoints (a species of prospective degradation, exploitation and subordination of women and possibly men) and participatory direct harms (current degradation, exploitation and subordination of women and possibly men). In other words, the *Labaye* Court unabashedly imported the Court's previous understandings of the offence and harm principles of jurisdiction and transmogrified them into its new harm principle for constituting criminal guilt. It would be rational to assume that the Court in *Labaye* used the *Prostitution Reference* to inform its species of harms as it mated those indicia with the community standards of tolerance test.

Regardless of whether this is an unhappy accident or purposeful importation, the result is a conflation of *constitutional jurisdiction* with construction of the *actus reus* (physical acts) of crime. The importation of the risk category into a test for criminal guilt allows a court the option of convicting someone on the basis of prospective risk using a standard of possibilities. Another way of thinking about this is that the obscene or indecent act in question *might* cause harm or *risks* causing harm; therefore, we'll nip it in the bud to prevent harm. This is much different from criminalizing conduct that has actually caused harm. Now that the notion of risk is deployed for establishing criminal indecency, decriminalization activists wish to see this same risk-based prudential logic inform the definition of prostitution, particularly when they call for prostitution-based offences to meet the harm principle under *Labaye* in order to establish criminal guilt (Craig 2008). In *Bedford v. Canada* (2010), we see liberal political values marshalled in the direction of limiting the power of the state to criminalize sex trade workers. The Court is calling upon Parliament to reconfigure the prostitution laws in such a way as to accord with its view of the proper functioning society based on social scientific evidence of harm to women. In either case, faux objective determination of what makes society function properly are deployed to better serve the power interests of women. The key difference between the legal challenge in *Bedford* and the pre-*Butler* case law is simply whose political perspective most influences what constitutes "proper" under the law. The idea that this is an achievable objective remains a fictional construct rooted in a Durkheimian world view (Pavlich 2011). Nevertheless, by relying upon the harm principle, decriminalization activists may convince the courts of their own interpretation of harm to women (which is a version of political morality) to effect law reform.

The decision creates a situation where aspects of the sex trade may be legalized in Ontario but may still be in force in other provinces. It also creates a situation where bawdy house prohibitions for the purposes of indecency which were deemed constitutional in *R. v. Labaye* [2005], but for the purposes of prostitution as a result of *Bedford v. Canada* [2010] would be unconstitutional in Ontario. The result would be piecemeal enforcement with considerable confusion as to why indecency-based offences (e.g., swingers clubs) remain constitutional while prostitution-based offences (e.g., brothels) violate the *Charter* (at least in Ontario).[3] After the decision, the federal government announced its intention to appeal and seek a further stay of Justice Himel's ruling. Justice Minister Rob Nicholson noted that prostitution is "a problem that harms individuals and communities" (Tibbets 2010). Nicholson had previously refused to consider the recommendation from the House of Commons Status of Women Committee to amend the laws and alter the enforcement of them to focus on those who exploit prostitutes rather than the actual sex trade workers.

Clearly, this creates considerable confusion for the enforcement of post-*Labaye* decisions across Canada and post-*Bedford v. Canada* (2010) cases in Ontario. This, combined with the Ontario court's apparent move to challenge the Supreme Court of Canada's earlier decision, makes this case an almost certain appellate case and one that is likely to meander its way to the Supreme Court. Certainly, the safety of sex trade workers in Canada is an important issue, but one could validly question whether courts are the best place to mete out complex social policy schemes. Those who oppose Justice Himel's decision will make compelling arguments about the discretion and institutional capacity of the Court (Manfredi and Kelly 2004: 744, 755). Manfredi and Kelly argue that cases such as these represent "judicial micro-management of public policy on the basis of poor evidence" (2004: 755) and that these sorts of cases rely on expertise "outside the traditional boundaries of judicial expertise and depend on subjective assessments of often conflicting social science evidence" (2004: 757). In short, they argue that Parliament is best equipped to deal with the regulation of prostitution and the Ontario court overstepped its traditional boundary by essentially re-administering the prostitution scheme.

What Happens When Harm Is Caused by Law?

What can be observed from the decriminalization arguments put before the courts is the attempt to marshal a harm principle as a means of justifying the decriminalization of sex work. While the courts have allowed the harm principle to determine the criminal act in the context of obscenity and indecency (*R. v. Labaye*), courts have been much less willing to use the same principle when citizens challenge laws. That is, courts have reconfigured laws in ways that allow for the exercise of power in more ambiguous terms, but they are much less willing to strike down law when citizens advance a harms-based argument. For example, amid the legalization of marijuana debate, the Supreme Court rejected the harm principle and the claim that the government had an obligation under s.7 of the *Charter* to demonstrate that the criminal law honours that principle. Victor Caine and David Malmo-Levine challenged the marijuana laws after they were both charged in separate incidents with possession of a narcotic and possession for the purposes of trafficking. The cases were heard together by the Supreme Court of Canada. Malmo-Levine is a Canadian "pot-activist" who has been seeking to decriminalize marijuana for years. He was arrested numerous times for "smoke-ins," in which he and his supporters protested the criminalization laws. He was eventually convicted for trafficking and took his constitutional challenge to the Supreme Court of Canada. Malmo-Levine argued that the laws against marijuana deprived persons who are sick and use marijuana for medicinal purposes of their section 7 guarantees (life, liberty and security of person) under the *Charter* by preventing them from obtaining treatment, and potentially imprisoning those who break the law. More broadly however, Malmo-Levine's position is similar to that taken by Bedford in that they both argue that the laws cause harm. Under s.7 Canadians have the right to "right to life, liberty and security of the person and the right not to be deprived thereof except in accordance with the principles of fundamental justice." Malmo-Levine argued that the law itself causes *harm* and reminded the Court that it is a principle of fundamental justice that a law should not cause harm. The Court disagreed with this position. In *R. v. Malmo-Levine; R. v. Caine* [2003], the majority of the Court argued that the harm principle is not a manageable standard by which to measure the deprivation of life, liberty or security of the person. In other words, the Court rejected the harm principle in the context of a *Charter* guarantee on the grounds that the harm principle was *not clear enough* to be a principle of fundamental justice. The reason for rejecting the harm-based argument was, according to the majority, that "harm can be marshalled on every side of virtually every criminal issue" (para. 127; Harcourt 1999: 113). Faced with seeing the marijuana law struck down, the Court refuses on the grounds that "we do not believe the content of the 'harm' principle, as described by Mill, and advocated by the appellants, provides a manageable standard under which to review criminal or other laws under s.7 of the *Charter*" (para. 129). However, when the state acts to protect us from harm through criminal sanction (as in *Labaye*), the harm principle is workable. In other words, harm is a "state interest" because the risk of harm from smoking marijuana to "vulnerable groups" is operationalized as "serious" and "substantial" (paras. 131–33). This pattern does not bode well for the litigants in *Bedford v. Canada* (2010), who seek to challenge the prostitution laws on similar grounds. Nevertheless, the harm principle *can* be marshalled both in favour of and against the decriminalization of prostitution. Whether the courts will view the harms caused by the legal regime to sex trade workers as more important than the harm caused to "vulnerable groups" who might be "lured by the wiles of a procurer" into the sex trade is purely a political question. However, given that courts have historically been concerned with the proper functioning of society, it is likely that the latter justification will take precedence over the former. Regardless of which side of the debate we examine, the courts can govern in either direction using the harm calculus. In the context of the sex trade, the Court has a long history of *tending* to govern in the direction of empowering the state rather than the individual. The anti-criminalization activists wish to seize these reigns and marshall the harm principle to the benefit of their cause. In either case, the governmental rationality operationalizes harm in a manner that tends to empower the state.

Notes

1. In other words, the client got the tug for free!
2. Not unlike the court's claim in *R. v. Pomeranov* (2007) where the "happy ending" was viewed as peripheral to the massage.
3. At the time of writing, this case is before the Court in Ontario. The government has asked for a continuation of Madame Justice Susan Himel's decision in which the prostitution laws were struck down but the law stayed for thirty days. The parties have agreed that that stay will remain in effect until the Court rules on the issue of the stay. The substantive issue of the constitutionality of the prostitution scheme will likely take many months, if not years, of litigation before this question reaches the Supreme Court of Canada.

Conclusion

Governing Through Harm

In chapter one of this book, we navigated a range of positions and debates around the use of law to promote liberal values in the area of obscenity and indecency. The conservative, liberal and various feminist justifications for and against state intervention were discussed. We were able to show that much of this legal debate is centred around political values and that the harm principle satisfies each of these values because it is an abstract category that can be filled with any particular meaning. In chapter two, we examined the case law leading up to the *Labaye* decision to show that the Court's work has always been a social technology aimed at maintaining a properly functioning society. The Court has seen its job as one where it protects a social order when that order is *threatened* or *harmed* by certain kinds of sexual images or conduct. These harms are framed as threats to liberal political principles such as liberty, autonomy and equality, which are presumed to exist as part of the normal functioning of society. In the Court's view, these political values are threatened by sexual representations and conduct which undermine society's proper functioning. The Court sees its job as one in which it protects society rather than as one where it promotes a particular political objective, whether framed in feminist, liberal or conservative terms. So, for example, equality is a state of society that already exists prior to the existence of obscenity or indecency, and that equality is to be secured by the state through law enforcement and criminal sanction. Thus is society's equilibrium is restored and liberal political values protected. In chapter three, we examined how this rationality is developed in the decision in *R. v. Labaye*. Here we discussed the effects of the Court's abandonment of the community standards of tolerance test to determine undue exploitation. They replaced the technology for determining obscenity and indecency with a harms-based test. Once the test for obscenity and indecency was de-coupled from the community — which the Court saw as sullied by political debate — they effectively depoliticized censorship by removing the test for criminalization from the context of political debate into the realm of abstraction. In theory, this facilitates the deployment of power from any political perspective. For this reason, it is no surprise that both the harm and risk of harm tests have been met with what Valverde (1999) described in the context of the *Butler* reconfiguration as "a warm reception by judges and the public." We have argued, along the same lines as Valverde (1999: 187), that "harms-based governance can have very different rationales and produce extremely varied effects." In chapter four, we examined the harm-based rationale in the context of case law relating to prostitution-based offences and their link to indecency law. The harm principle in the context of prostitution has been deployed by the courts to justify criminalization (*Prostitution Reference* 1990). More recently, a lower court in Ontario has accepted the harm principle as a means of striking down the prostitution-based laws, agreeing with the anti-criminalization feminist movement's claim that the law causes harm to women. In both cases, harm is the principal technology of governance. Ultimately, it is the courts that determine the interpretation of harm, but this continues to be a political exercise that will remain before the courts until the Supreme Court declares the laws unconstitutional or until Parliament takes legislative action. Lawyers will always see a distinction between the harm principle deployed for the purpose of justifying state intervention (constitutionality) versus the harm principle deployed to establish criminal guilt (*actus reus*). We recognize the different legal burdens and onuses that inure in law; however, the fundamental philosophy underpinning the use of the harm principle in either situation is apposite. Regardless of whether the Court considers the justifiability of law versus criminal guilt, their consideration of harm focuses on the proper functioning of society.

Currently, the Supreme Court of Canada seems to be most interested, when it makes a finding of indecency or obscenity, in the *proper functioning of society*. The *Labaye* Court determined that this functionalism can best be established when we criminalize conduct which is harmful or which carries a risk of harm; yet the categories that the Court creates as species of harms are not necessarily in accordance with traditional liberal understandings of harm that justify state intervention. Few would dispute the notion that non-consensual sexual acts cause harm. However, the Court's categories of attitudinal change to the viewer and incursions to a passerby's liberty seem more amorphous and incapable of quantification. Drawing on its previous obscenity and indecency canon, it seems clear that when the Court speaks of attitudinal change it is most worried about *Butler* categories of harm — that is, materials that are degrading and dehumanizing to women and that have a significant risk of harm typically constitute criminal guilt. Similarly, sexuality paired with depictions of violence and horror are viewed by the courts as harmful to society under the *Labaye* formulation. When the Court speaks of attitudinal harm, it is concerned primarily with materials that might cause attitudes to change resulting in anti-social acts that might "harm" society. This is a neoliberal iteration of harm because it is only concerned with harms to "worthy" populations; in *Labaye*, these "worthy" populations seem to be harmless passersby and those who are not already predisposed to swinging.

Thus, when the Court speaks of harm, inherent in this conception is a tacit caveat; it would appear the Court is mostly concerned with materials and conduct that *further* "harm" society. In *Labaye*, it seems presumptive that the reason no one was "attitudinally changed" in the swinger's club was because the participants, particularly the women, were already predisposed to an "unruly" sexual practice (i.e., swinging). When the Court switches its analysis to affronts to liberty, the Court finds that the measures the club took were enough to keep the activities inside and away from the harmless passerby. Presumably, that passerby, if confronted with the activities of the club, could experience attitudinal change but just as importantly might be affronted by the activities. In this manner, the Court interlinks the notions of equality and liberty as values that can be compromised by obscenity and indecency; thus criminalizing conduct which offends these constitutional values offers the Court a way out of the political mire it found itself in throughout the 1990s.

Certainly, the decision in *Labaye* has been met with some optimism in recent feminist scholarship (Craig 2008). More recently Craig has argued that *Labaye* is an example of a court that is conceding that sex could be and even should be pleasurable: "The reasoning in *Labaye* thus protects our common interests in tolerance and human flourishing, achieved through the recognition and affirmation of sexual pleasure, bound by both sexual dissent and liberal judgment" (Craig 2009: 385). Grounding her analysis in classical liberal legal theory, Craig frames her contentions by noting that "Oh, and one last thing. You need not worry anymore about police raids [at the swinger's clubs]" (357).

We remain unconvinced by those who would argue that the harm test is sexually emancipatory. In the first instance, the reasoning is specious because it reduces a legal decision's meaning to its disposition — whether or not an individual is criminalized in a particular case context. Thus, the argument equates the legalization of swinger's clubs in some contexts with sexual liberty for all, despite the fact that the club was shut down for almost a year. Such an analysis also ignores the broader discursive effects of law. Thus, where some might view the harm test as liberatory, we would urge the reader to interrogate more fully the subtexts of the Court's reasoning. One could see *Labaye* as a victory for feminism because it allows for more sexual freedom albeit in private spaces. One could also read *Labaye* and see a Court that views sexuality as dangerous and something to be inoculated from — hence, we will allow only the predisposed to partake in unruly sexually practices and only when they do so in a sufficiently private space. The analytic means that we have no recourse to care about what vulnerable or minority populations may have to say about their own forms of sexual expression; we mute the voices of those who might advocate for freer sexuality in the service of "objective" harms such as attitudinal change and affronts to liberty. The objective analysis means that sexuality as a site of multiplicity and complexity can always be reduced to intolerable and therefore criminalizable.

It matters not, for instance, that materials (which might contain some violent depictions), addressed in cases such as *Little Sisters*, might be viewed as tolerable or even desirable in queer communities, but rather that such materials be kept out of mainstream society and be limited to only those who are attitudinally changed — i.e., queer men and women. The voices of such communities are quieted as the rhetoric of risk of harm increases. If we wish to avoid affronts and attitudinal change, their voices are discredited for being "political" because they reflect self-interest. Rather, what matters is the voice of the Court, and after all, is not the Court best situated to speak to liberty and equality in a constitutional democracy? Of course, such reasoning is circular; it presumes liberty and equality because the Court is the guardian of the *Constitution*, which itself contains a liberty and equality guarantee. The reasoning here is also self-serving because the Court drafts a new harm test and then itself adjudicates the test on its merits. Such inoculation is cold comfort to those amongst us who view the Court through the prism of discursive analysis and in light of the history of obscenity and indecency law. In *Labaye*, we see neither the enshrinement of liberty nor the incremental embrace of sex as pleasurable in the Court's "harm" calculus.

In *Labaye*, the Supreme Court has elucidated an equivocated harm principle, one which constitutes criminal guilt, when the principle would, in the name of jurisprudential consistency, establish criminal jurisdiction. The price paid for such a jurisprudential turn is more than discursive. The price paid serves the usual functionalism that such moralistic contortion requires. In the context of obscenity and indecency, the Court is most interested in "the proper functioning of society." The price paid includes the muting of equality interests as less central in the harm debate and results in a universalized abstraction of legal subjects — an abstraction that is less rich in the politics of recognition from previous iterations of legal tests for obscenity and indecency. Lastly, *Labaye* represents the enshrinement of a principle of harm for the purposes of establishing guilt rather than merely authorizing Parliament's power to make law (as in the *Prostitution Reference*). Ultimately, the meaning of this discursive shift is old functionalism in new illiberal attire, and its constitution and reflection into society will be meted out by future jurisprudence and governmental action. Those decisions will likely be problematized in the years to come, as we continue to interrogate what has become of the new harm principle.

References

Bakan, Joel. 1997. *Just Words: Constitutional Rights and Social Wrongs*. Toronto: University of Toronto Press.

Bourricaud, F. 1981. *The Sociology of Talcott Parsons* Chicago: University of Chicago Press.

Barry, Andrew, Thomas Osborne and Nikolas Rose (eds.). 1996. *Foucault and Political Reason: Liberalism, Neoliberalism and Rationalites of Government*. Chicago: University of Chicago Press.

Barry, Kathleen. 1995. *The Prostitution of Sexuality* New York: New York University Press.

Bauman, Zygmunt. 2000. "Social Uses of Law and Order." In David Garland and Richard Sparks (eds.), *Criminology and Social Theory*. Oxford: Oxford University Press.

BCCLA (British Columbia Civil Liberties Association). 1992. "Factum of the Intervener." In *R. v. Butler* [1992] 1 S.C.R. 452. Supreme Court of Canada.

_____. 2006. "BCCLA Position Paper: Sexuality and Civil Rights: Freedom from Government Reprisal." <www.bccla.org/lbgtq.html>.

Bell, Shannon. 1997. "On ne peut pas voir l'image [The image cannot be seen]. In Brenda Cossman, Shannon Bell, Lise Gotell, and Becki L. Ross (eds.), *Bad Attitude/s on Trial: Pornography, Feminism and the Butler Decision*. Toronto: University of Toronto Press.

Benedet, Janine. 2001. "Little Sisters Book and Art Emporium v. Minister of Justice: Sex Equality and the Attack on R. v. Butler." *Osgoode Hall Law Journal* 39: 187–205.

Benhabib, Seyla. 1992. *Situating the Self: Gender, Community and Postmodernism in Contemporary Ethics*. New York: Routledge.

Benhabib, Seyla, Drucilla Cornell and Nancy Fraser (eds.). 1995. *Feminist Contentions*. London: Routledge.

Boyce, Bret. 2008. "Obscenity and Community Standards." *Yale Journal of International Law* 33: 299–368.

Brown, Wendy. 2000. "The Mirror of Pornography." In Drucilla Cornell (ed.). *Feminism and Pornography*. Oxford: Oxford University Press.

Burstyn, Varda (ed.). 1985. *Women Against Censorship.* Toronto: Douglas and MacIntyre.

Busby, Karen. 1993. "LEAF and Pornography: Litigating on Equality and Sexual Representations." Position paper of the Women's Legal Education Action Fund.

_____. 1994. "LEAF and Pornography: Litigating on Equality and Sexual Representations." *Canadian Journal of Law and Society* 9: 165–92.

_____. 2004. "The Queer Sensitive Interveners in the Little Sisters Case: A Response to Dr. Kendall." In Todd G. Morrison (ed.), *Eclectic Views on Gay Male Pornography: Pornucopia* Binghamton, NY: Harrington Park Press.

Castel, R. 1991. "From Dangerousness to Risk." In G. Burchell, C. Gordon and P. Miller (eds.), *The Foucault Effect: Studies in Governmentality*. Chicago: University of Chicago Press.

Chapkis, Wendy. 1998. *Live Sex Acts: Women Performing Erotic Labour*. New York: Routledge.

Clear, T., and E. Cadora. 2001. "Risk and Community Practice." In K. Stenson and R.R. Sullivan (eds.), *Crime, Risk and Justice: The Politics of Crime Control in Liberal Democracies*, Cullompton: Willan Publishing.

Cole, Susan. 1989. *Pornography and the Sex Crisis*. Toronto: Amanita Press.

Cornell, Drucilla. 1991. *Beyond Accommodation: Ethical Feminism, Deconstruction and the Law*. London: Routledge.

Cossman, Brenda. 1997. "Feminist Fashion or Morality in Drag? The Sexual Subtext of the Butler Decision." In Brenda Cossman, Shannon Bell, Lise Gotell, and Becki L. Ross (eds.), *Bad Attitude/s on Trial: Pornography, Feminism and the Butler Decision*. Toronto: University of Toronto Press.

_____. 2003. "Disciplining the Unruly: Sexual Outlaws, Little Sisters and the Legacy of Butler." *University of British Columbia Law Review* 36: 77–99.

_____. 2004. "Sexuality, Queer Theory, and 'Feminism After': Reading and Rereading the Sexual Subject." *McGill Law Journal* 49: 847–51.

_____. 2007. *Sexual Citizens: The Legal and Cultural Regulation of Sex and Belonging*. Stanford, CA: Stanford University Press.

Cossman, Brenda, and Shannon Bell. 1997. "Introduction." In Brenda Cossman, Shannon Bell, Lise Gotell, and Becki L. Ross (eds.), *Bad Attitude/s on Trial: Pornography, Feminism and the Butler Decision*. Toronto: University of Toronto Press.

Cossman, Brenda, Shannon Bell, Lise Gotell, and Becki L. Ross (eds.). 1997. *Bad Attitude/s on Trial: Pornography, Feminism and the Butler Decision*. Toronto: University of Toronto Press.

Craig, Elaine. 2008. "Re-interpreting the Criminal Regulation of Sew Work in Light of R. v. Labaye." *Canadian Criminal Law Review* 12(3): 327–51.

_____. 2009. "Laws of Desire: The Political Morality of Public Sex." *McGill Law Journal* 54: 355–85.

Dean, Mitchell. 1999. *Governmentality: Power and Rule in Modern Society*. London: Sage Publications.

Delacoste, Frederique, and Priscilla Alexander. 1988. *Sex Work: Writings by Women in the Sex Industry*. London: Virago.

Deva, Jim. 2006. <www.littlesisters.ca/docscc/index_court.html>.

Dworkin, Andrea. 1998. "Against the Male Flood: Censorship, Pornography, and Equality." In Robert E. Baird and Stuart E. Rosenbaum (eds.), *Pornography: Private Right or Public Menace?* New York: Prometheus Books.

Dworkin, Ronald. 1978. *Taking Rights Seriously*. Cambridge: Harvard University Press.

_____. 1980. "Is the Press Losing the First Amendment?" *New York Review of Books* 49.

_____. 1993. "Women and Pornography." *New York Review of Books* 21.

Easton, Susan M. 1994. *The Problem of Pornography: Regulation and the Right to Free Speech*. London: Routledge.

Editorial. "Reading Between the Borderlines." *Globe and Mail* (June 30, 1992) A16.

Farley, Melissa. 1998. "Prostitution, Violence, and Posttraumatic Stress Disorder" *Women and Health* 27(3).

Feinberg, Joel. 1984. *Harm to Others (The Moral Limits of the Criminal Law)*. Volume 1. New York: Oxford University Press.

_____. 1985. *Offence to Others (The Moral Limits of the Criminal Law)*. Volume 2. New York: Oxford University Press.

Fish, A. 1989. "Hate Promotion and Freedom of Expression: Truth and Consequences." *Canadian Journal of Law & Jurisprudence* 2: 111.

Fish, Stanley. 2008. *Save The World on Your Own Time*. Oxford: Oxford University Press.

Fisher, John. 2004. "Outlaws or In-laws? Successes and Challenges in the Struggle for LGBT Equality." *McGill Law Journal* 49: 1183–208.

Foucault, Michel. 1980. *Power/Knowledge: Selected Interviews and Other Writings 1972–1977*. Edited by Colin Gordon. London: Harvester.

_____. 1991. "Governmentality." Trans. Rosi Braidotti and revised by Colin Gordon. In Graham Burchell, Colin Gordon and Peter Miller (eds.), *The Foucault Effect: Studies in Governmentality*. Chicago, IL: University of Chicago Press.

_____. 1994. "Security, Territory, Population." In Paul Rabinow and Nikolas Rose (eds.), *The Essential Foucault: Selections from Essential Works of Foucault, 1954–1984*. New York: New Press.

_____. 1997. *"Society Must Be Defended": Lectures at the Collège de France 1975–1976*. Mauro Bertani and Alessandro Fontana (eds.), translated by David Macey. New York: Picador.

Fraser Report. 1985. *Canada, Pornography and Prostitution in Canada, Volume II*. Special Committee on Pornography and Prostitution (Fraser Committee) Ottawa: Department of Supply and Services.

Garland, David. 1997. "'Governmentality' and the Problem of Crime: Foucault, Criminology, Sociology." *Theoretical Criminology* 1(2): 173–214.

Golder, Ben, and Peter Fitzpatrick. 2009. *Foucault's Law*. London: Routledge.

Gordon, Colin. 1991. "Governmental Rationality: An Introduction." In Graham Burchell, Colin Gordon and Peter Miller (eds.), *The Foucault Effect: Studies in Governmentality*. Chicago, IL: University of Chicago Press.

Gotell, Lise. 1997. "Shaping Butler: The New Politics of Anti-Pornography." In Brenda Cossman, Shannon Bell, Lise Gotell, and Becki L. Ross (eds.), *Bad Attitude/s on Trial: Pornography, Feminism and the Butler Decision*. Toronto: University of Toronto Press.

Green, Leslie. 2000. "Pornographies." *Journal of Political Philosophy* 27.

_____. 2006. "Men in the Place of Women, from Butler to Little Sisters." *Osgoode Hall Law Journal* 43: 473.

Gorkoff, Kelly, and Jane Runner (eds.). 2003. *Being Heard: The Experiences of Young Women in Prostitution*. Halifax & Winnipeg: Fernwood Publishing.

Grosghal, J., "When is Free Speech Hate Speech?" *McGill Tribune* (27 March 2001), online: <http://media.www.mcgilltribune.com/media/storage/paper234/news/2001/03/27/News/When-Is.Free.Speech.Hate.Speech-59065.shtml.>.

Hanger, Art, and John Maloney. 2006. "The Challenge of Change: A Study of Canada's Criminal Prostitution Laws: A Report of the Standing Committees on Justice and Human Right and the Subcommittee on Solicitation Laws." Ottawa: Government of Canada. <http://www2.parl.gc.ca/content/hoc/

Committee/391/JUST/Reports/RP2599932/justrp06/sslrrp06-e.pdf>.

Harcourt, Bernard E. 1999. "The Collapse of the Harm Principle." *The Journal of Criminal Law & Criminology* 90: 109–94.

Harris, Angela P. 2006. "From Stonewall to the Suburbs? Toward a Political Economy of Sexuality." *William and Mary Bill of Rights Journal* 14: 1539–82.

Hudson, Barbara. 2003. *Justice in the Risk Society.* London: Sage Publications.

Hunt, Alan, and Gary Wickham. 1994. *Foucault and Law: Towards a Sociology of Law as Governance.* London: Pluto Press.

Hunt, Lynn. 2000. "Obscenity and the Origins of Modernity, 1500–1800." In Drucilla Cornell (ed.), *Feminism and Pornography.* Oxford: Oxford University Press.

Hutchinson, Allan C. 1995. "In Other Words: Putting Sex and Pornography in Context." *Canadian Journal of Law and Jurisprudence* 8: 107–38.

Jochelson, Richard. 2009a. "After *Labaye*: The Harm Test of Obscenity, the New Judicial Vacuum and the Relevance of Familiar Voices." *Alberta Law Review* 46 (3): 741–68.

_____. 2009b. "*R. v. Labaye*: The Fogginess of 'Increased' Causality in Obscenity Law." *Alberta Law Review* (Supplement February Edition: 1–10).

Johnson, Kirsten. 1995. *Undressing the Canadian State: The Politics of Pornography from Hicklin to Butler.* Halifax, NS: Fernwood Publishing.

_____. 1999. "Obscenity, Gender and the Law." In Elizabeth Comack (ed.), *Locating Law: Race/Class/Gender Connections.* Halifax, NS: Fernwood Publishing.

Kendall, Christopher N. 2004a. *Gay Male Pornography: An Issue of Sex Discrimination.* Vancouver: University of British Columbia Press.

_____. 2004b. "Gay Male Pornography and Sexual Violence: A Sex Equality Perspective on Gay Male Rape and Partner Abuse." *McGill Law Journal* 49: 877–923.

Koppelman, Andrew. 2005. "Does Obscenity Cause Moral Harm?" *Columbia Law Review* 105: 1635–79.

_____. 2006. "Reading Lolita at Guantánamo: Or, This Page Cannot Be Displayed." *Dissent* Spring 53(2): 64–71.

_____. 2008. "Why Phyllis Schlafly Is Right (But Wrong) About Pornography" *Harvard Journal of Law and Public Policy* 31: 107–25.

Kramar, Kirsten. 2006. "Victims of Justice: Ageism and Whorephobia." In Elizabeth Comack (ed.), *Locating Law: Race/Class/Gender/Sexuality Connections.* Halifax and Winnipeg: Fernwood Publishing.

Kuhn, Annette A. 1985. *The Power of Image: Essays on Representation and Sexuality.* London: Routledge.

LEAF. 2000. Media Release. "Supreme Court Issues Decision in Little Sisters Response of the Women's Legal Education and Action Fund." <www.leaf.ca/media/releases.html#target>.

Lewis, Jacqueline, and Eleanor Maticka-Tyndale. 2000, "Licensing Sex Work: Public Policy and Women's Lives." *Canadian Public Policy* 26(4): 437. <qed.econ.queensu.ca/pub/cpp/Dec2000/Lewis.pdf>.

Lacombe, Dany. 1994. *Blue Politics: Pornography and the Law in the Age of Feminism.* Toronto: University of Toronto Press.

Langton, Rae. 1993. "Speech Acts and Unspeakable Acts." *Philosophy and Public Affairs* 22(4): 293.

Lederer, Laura. 1980. "Pornography, Oppression, and Freedom: A Closer Look." In Laura Lederer (ed.), *Take Back the Night*. New York: William Morrow.

Lemke, Thomas. 2000. "Foucault, Governmentality and Critique." Paper presented at the RethinkingMarxism Conference, University of Amherst MA, September 21–24.

_____. 2002. "Foucault, Governmentality, and Critique." *Rethinking Marxism* 14(3): 49–64.

Lessig, L. 1995. "The Regulation of Social Meaning." *University of Chicago Law Review* 62(3): 943.

Litowitz, D.E. 1997. *Postmodern Philosophy and Law*. Lawrence, KS: University Press of Kansas.

Longino, H.E. 1998. "Pornography, Oppression and Freedom: A Closer Look." In Robert E. Baird and Stuart E. Rosenbaum (eds.), *Pornography: Private Right or Public Menace?* New York: Prometheus Books.

Lowman, John. 2000. "Violence and the Outlaw Status of (Street) Prostitution in Canada." *Violence Against Women* 6(9): 998.

_____. 2009. "Deadly Inertia: A History of Constitutional Challenges to Canada's Criminal Code Sections on Prostitution." <http://mypage.uniserve.ca/~lowman/>.

_____. 1998. "Prostitution Law Reform in Canada." *Toward Comparative Law in the 21st Century*. Edited by the Institute of Comparative Law in Japan. Tokyo: Chuo University Press.

MacKinnon, Catharine A. 1985. "Pornography, Civil Rights, and Speech." *Harvard Civil Rights—Civil Liberties Law Review* 20: 1–70.

_____. 1987. *Feminism Unmodified*. Cambridge, MA: Harvard University Press.

_____. 1993. *Only Words*. Cambridge, MA: Harvard University Press.

_____. 2003. *Sex Equality: Sexual Harassment*. New York: Foundation Press.

_____. 2007 "Pornography as Trafficking." In David E. Guinn (ed.), *Pornography: Driving the Demand in International Sex Trafficking*. Los Angeles: Captive Daughters Media.

Mahoney, K. 1991. "Canaries in a Coalmine: Canadian Judges and the Reconstruction of the Obscenity Law." In David Schneiderman (ed.), *Freedom of Expression and the Charter*. Toronto: Thomson.

Makin, Kirk. 2010. "Judge Decriminalizes Prostitution in Ontario, but Ottawa Mulls Appeal." *Globe and Mail*, September 28.

Malarek, Victor. 2003. *The Natashas: The New Global Sex Trade*. Toronto: Penguin.

Manfredi, Christopher, and James B. Kelly. 2004. "Misrepresenting the Supreme Court's Record? A Comment on Sujit Choudhry and Claire E. Hunter, 'Measuring Judicial Activism on the Supreme Court of Canada.'" *McGill Law Journal* 49.

Mathen, Carissima. 2001. "Little Sisters v. Canada." *National Journal of Constitutional Law* 13: 165–81.

McLaren, Angus, and Arlene Tiger McLaren. 1986. *The Bedroom and the State: The Changing Practices and Politics of Contraception and Abortion in Canada, 1880–1996*. The Canadian Social History Series. Toronto: McClelland and Stewart.

McLaren, John. 1985. "Chasing the Social Evil: Moral Fervor and the Evolution of Canada's Prostitution Laws: 1867–1917." *Canadian Journal of Law and Society*

1(1): 136.

Meiklejohn, A. 1961. "The First Amendment is an Absolute." *University of Chicago Press Supreme Court Review.*

Mill, John, Stuart. 1869. *On Liberty.* <www.bartleby.com/130>.

Mirza, Ahan. 2009. "Foucault's Law, by Ben Golder and Peter Fitzpatrick." *Osgoode Hall Law Journal* 47: 617–18.

Moon, Richard. 1985. "The Scope of Freedom of Expression." *Osgoode Hall Law Journal* 23: 331.

_____. 2000. *The Constitutional Protection of Freedom of Expression.* Toronto: University of Toronto Press.

_____. 2002. "Justified Limits on Free Expression: The Collapse of the General Approach to Limits on Charter Rights." *Osgoode Hall Law Journal* 40: 337.

Noonan, S. 1985. "Pornography: Preferring the Feminist Approach of the British Columbia Court of Appeal to that of the Fraser Committee." *Criminal Reports* (3d) 45: 61–68.

Nowlin Christopher. 2003. *Judging Obscenity: A Critical History of Expert Evidence* Montreal: McGill-Queens University Press.

Nussbaum, Martha C. 1999. *Sex and Social Justice.* New York: Oxford University Press.

Nussbaum, Martha C., and Teela Sanders. 2005. "It's Just Acting: Sex Workers' Strategies for Capitalizing on Sexuality." *Gender, Work and Organization* 12(4): 319.

O'Connell Davidson, Julia. 1998. *Prostitution, Power and Freedom.* Ann Arbor: University of Michigan.

O'Malley, Pat. 1996. "Risk and Responsibility." In Andrew Barry, Thomas Osborne and Nikolas Rose (eds.), *Foucault and Political Reason: Liberalism, Neoliberalism and Rationalites of Government.* Chicago: University of Chicago Press.

_____. 2004. *Risk, Uncertainty and Government.* London: Glasshouse Press.

Ost, Suzanne. 2009. *Child Pornography and Sexual Grooming: Legal and Societal Responses.* Cambridge: Cambridge University Press.

Pavilich, George. 2011. *Law & Society Redefined.* London: Oxford University Press.

Peart, Sandra J., and David M. Levy. 2008. "Darwin's Unpublished Letter at the Bradlaugh–Besant Trial." *European Journal of Political Economy* 24: 343–53.

Pickel, Jo-Anne. 2001. "Taking Big Brother to Court: Little Sisters Book and Art Emporium v. Canada (Minister of Justice)." *University of Toronto Faculty of Law Review* 59: 349–66.

Pivot Legal Society, Sex Work Subcommittee. 2004. "Voices for Dignity: A Call to End the Harms Caused by Canada's Sex Trade Laws." <pivotlegal.org/Publications/reportsvfd.htm>.

Polak, M., "Guess Who's Watching Porn." *Macleans Magazine* 121, 25: 2 (June 30, 2008).

Post, R.C. 1991. "Free Speech and Religious, Racial, and Sexual Harassment: Racist Speech, Democracy and the First Amendment." Wm. & Mary L. Rev. 32: 267.

Poulantzas, N. 2000. *State, Power, Socialism.* Trans. Patrick Camiller. London: Verso.

Raymond, Janice. 1998. "Prostitution as Violence against Women: NGO Stonewalling in Beijing and Elsewhere." *Women's Studies International Forum* 21(1).

Rose, Nikolas. 1999. *Governing the Soul: The Shaping of the Private Self.* London: Free Associations Books.

Rose, Nikolas, Pat O'Malley, and Mariana Valverde. 2006. "Governmentality." *Annual*

Review of Law and Social Science 2: 83–104.

Rose Nikolas, and Mariana Valverde. 1998. "Governed by Law?" *Social & Legal Studies* 7: 541–51.

Ross, Becki L. 1997. "'It's Merely Designed for Sexual Arousal': Interrogating the Indefensibility of Lesbian Smut." In Brenda Cossman, Shannon Bell, Lise Gotell, and Becki L. Ross (eds.), *Bad Attitude/s on Trial: Pornography, Feminism and the Butler Decision*. Toronto: University of Toronto Press.

Ryder, Bruce. 2001. "The Little Sisters Case, Administrative Censorship, and Obscenity Law." *Osgoode Hall Law Journal* 39: 207–27.

_____. 2003. "The Harms of Child Pornography." *University of British Columbia Law Review* 36: 101–35.

Sanders, Teela. 2005. "It's Just Acting: Sex Workers' Strategies for Capitalizing on Sexuality." *Gender, Work and Organization* 12(4): 319.

Scales, Ann. 1994. "Avoiding Constitutional Depression: Bad Attitudes and the Fate of *Butler.*" *Canadian Journal of Women and the Law* 7(2): 349–92.

Scanlon, T.M. 1972. "A Theory of Freedom of Expression." *Philosophy & Public Affairs* 1: 204.

Segal, Lynne, and Mary McIntosh. 1993. *Sex Exposed: Sexuality and the Pornography Debate*. Rutgers: Rutgers University Press.

Sex TV, Episode 2-07, *On Our Backs* Magazine, Original Air Date: Saturday, November 27, 1999, Pedro Orrego, Producer.

Shaver, Frances M. 1988. "A Critique of the Feminist Charges against Prostitution." *Atlantis* 4(1): 82

Smart, Carol. 1989. *Feminism and the Power of Law*. New York: Routledge.

Smith, Russell 2010. "Rémy Couture's Violent Videos Are Dumb, but That's not Illegal." <theglobeandmail.com/news/arts/russell-smith/rmy-coutures-violent-videos-are-dumb-but-thats-not-illegal/article1765624>. October 20.

Smith, Steven, D. 1987. "Skepticism, Tolerance, and Truth in the Theory of Free Expression." *Southern California Law Review* 60: 49.

_____. 2004. "The Hollowness of the Harm Principle." University of San Diego Legal Studies Research Paper No. 05-07: Paper 17. <http://law.bepress.com/cgi/viewcontent.cgi?article=1021&context=sandiegolwps.d>.

_____. 2006. "Is the Harm Principle Illiberal?" *The American Journal of Jurisprudence* 51: 1–42.

Stenson, K., and R.R. Sullivan (eds.). 2001. *Crime, Risk and Justice: The Politics of Crime Control in Liberal Democracies*, Cullompton: Willan Publishing.

Strossen, Nadine. 1995. *Defending Pornography*. New York: Anchor Books Doubleday.

Sumner, Wayne, L. 2004. *The Hateful and the Obscene: Studies in the Limits of Free Expression*. Toronto: University of Toronto Press.

Sunstein, Cass. 1993. *Democracy and the Problem of Free Speech*. New York: Free Press.

Tibbetts, Janice. 2010. "Ottawa to Appeal Ontario Court's Prostitution Ruling." *National Post*, Sept. 29.

Valverde, Mariana. 1991. *Age of Light, Soap and Water: Moral Reform in Canada, 1885–1925*. Toronto: McClelland and Stewart.

_____. 1999. "The Harms of Sex and the Risks of Breasts: Obscenity and Indecency in Canadian Law." *Social & Legal Studies* 8: 181–97.

_____. 2003. *Law's Dream of a Common Knowledge*. Princeton and Oxford: Princeton

University Press.

van der Meulen, Emily, and Elya Maria Durisin. 2008. "Why Decriminalize? How Canada's Municipal and Federal Regulations Increase Sex Workers' Vulnerability." *Canadian Journal of Women and the Law* 20(2): 289–311.

Waltman, Max. 2010. "United States Rethinking Democracy: Legal Challenges to Pornography and Sex Inequality in Canada and the United States." *Political Research Quarterly* 63: 218.

Weitzer, Ronald. 2005. "Flawed Theory and Method in Studies of Prostitution." *Violence Against Women* 11(7).

Young, Alan. 2008. "The State Is Still in the Bedrooms of the Nation: The Control and Regulation of Sexuality in Canadian Criminal Law." *The Canadian Journal of Human Sexuality* 17(4): 203–20.

Young, Diana. 2008. "Claims for Recognition and the Generalized Other: The Reasonable Person and Judgment in Criminal Law." *Canadian Journal of Law and Society* 23: 16–37.

Young, Iris M. 1990. *Justice and the Politics of Difference*. Princeton: Princeton University Press.

Zanghellini, Aleardo. 2004. "Is Little Sisters Just Butler's Little Sister?" *University of British Columbia Law Review* 37: 407–48.

Statutes

Canadian Charter of Rights and Freedoms, Part I of the *Constitution Act*, 1982, being Schedule B to the *Canada Act* 1982 (U.K.), 1982, c. 11.

Criminal Code of Canada, R.S.C. 1985, c. C-46.

Customs Act, R.S.C. 1985 (2nd Supp.) c. 1.

Customs Tariff, S.C. 1987, c. 49, Sch. VII, Code 9956(a) (now S.C. 1997, c. 36. s. 166, Sch., Tariff Item 9899.00.00).

Case Law

Bedford v. Canada (2010) ONSC 4264

Conway v. The King 1944 2 D.L.R. 530

Glad Day Bookshop Inc. v. Deputy Minister of National Revenue (Customs & Excise) (July 14, 1992), 1992 CarswellOnt 2665, [1992] O.J. No. 1466 Doc. 619/90 (Ont. Gen. Div.).

Irwin Toy Ltd. v. Quebec (Attorney General), [1989] 1 S.C.R. 927

Little Sisters Book and Art Emporium v. Canada (Minister of Justice), [1996] B.C.J. No. 71. (Sup. Ct.).

Little Sisters Book and Art Emporium v. Canada, [2000] 2 S.C.R. 1120.

R. v. Bedford [2000] O.J. No. 887,

R. v. Blais-Pelletier, [1999] 3 S.C.R. 863.

R. v. Brodie, [1962] S.C.R. 681, 32 D.L.R. (2d).

R. v. Butler, [1992] 1 S.C.R. 452.

R. v. Colalillo, [2006] Carswell Que 546 (Qb. Sup. Ct).

R. v. Dominion News & Gifts, (1963), 42 W.W.R. 65, 2 C.C.C. 103

R. v. Dominion News & Gifts, [1964] S.C.R. 251.

R. v. Ellison, [2006] B.C.J. No. 3241, 2006 BCPC 549.

R. v. Erotica Video Exchange Ltd., (1994), 163 A.R. 181 (Prov. Ct.).

R. v. Glad Day Bookshops Inc. 70 O.R. (3d) 691 • 239 D.L.R. (4th) 119 • 183 C.C.C. (3d) 449 • 118 C.R.R. (2d) 209

R. v. Hawkins, (1993), 15 O.R. (3d) 549 (C.A.).

R. v. Hicklin, (1868), 3 LR.Q.B. 360.

R. v. Jacob, (1996), 112 C.C.C. (3d) 1 (Ont. C.A.).

R. v. Jorgensen, [1995] 4 S.C.R. 55; [1995] S.C.J. No. 92.

R. v. Jorgensen et al., 15 O.R. (3d) 549; [1993] O.J. No. 2572 (C.A.).

R. v. Keegstra, [1990] 3 S.C.R. 697.

R. v. Kouri, [2005] 3 S.C.R. 789, [2005] S.C.J. No. 82.

R. v. Labaye, [2005] 3 S.C.R. 728.

R. v. Malmo-Levine; R. v. Caine, [2003] 3 S.C.R. 571, 2003 SCC 74

R. v. Mara, [1997] 2 S.C.R. 630

R. v. Martin Secker Warburg Ltd. And Others 2 E. R. 683

R. v. Mohan, [1994] 2 S.C.R. 9

R. v. National News, (1953) 106 C.C.C. 26

R. v. Oakes, [1986] S.C.J. No. 7.

R. v. Ponomarev, [2007] O.J. No. 2494, 2007 ONCJ 271.

R. v. Red Hot Video (1985) 45 C. R. 3(d) 36 (B.C.C.A)

R. v. Ronish (1993), 26 C.R. (4th) 75.

R v. Ronish et al. [1993] O.J. No. 2572

R. v. Scythes, [1993] O.J. No. 537.

R. v. Sharpe, [2001] 1 S.C.R. 45.

R. v. Sheikh, [2008] O.J. No. 1544 (ON S.C.)

R. v. Towne Cinema Theatres Ltd., [1985] 1 S.C.R. 494, 18 D.L.R. (4th) 1.

R. v. Tremblay, [1993] 2 S.C.R. 932

R. v. Wagner (1985) 43 C. R. 3(d) 318 (Alta Q.B.)

Reference re ss. 193 & 195.1(1)(c) of Criminal Code (Canada), (the Prostitution Reference), [1990] 1 S.C.R. 1123.

Towne Cinema Theatres Ltd. v. The Queen [1985] 1 S.C.R. 494

Supreme Court Facta/Briefs

Little Sisters Book and Art Emporium v. Canada (Minister of Justice), [2000] 2 S.C.R.1120 (Factum of the Intervener, EGALE). Date of publication 1999.

Little Sisters Book and Art Emporium v. Canada (Minister of Justice), [2000] 2 S.C.R.1120 (Factum of the Intervener, Equality Now). Date of publication 1999.

Little Sisters Book and Art Emporium v. Canada (Minister of Justice), [2000] 2 S.C.R.1120 (Factum of the Intervener, Women's Legal, Education and Action Fund). Date of publication 1999.

R v. Butler, [1992] 1 S.C.R. 452 1, (Factum of the Intervener, the British Columbia Civil Liberties Association).

R v. Butler, [1992] 1 S.C.R. 452 (Factum of the Intervener, Women's Legal, Education and Action Fund).